To JOE & ROSE   26 APRIL 91

MAY ALL YOUR DREAMS
BE GREAT ONES

KEEP ON CRICKEN

Also by Jay Hirsch

The Last Convertibles
Great American Dream Machines

More
Great American
Dream
Machines

More Great American Dream Machines

Text and Photos by Jay Hirsch

Random House New York

Page iii: 1953 *Buick V-8 engine compartment. Owner: Gary Rabinowitz/NY*
Page iv: 1950 *Plymouth Station Wagon. Owner: Ernest Fodor/NJ*

Copyright © 1990 by Jay Hirsch

All rights reserved under International and Pan-American Copyright Conventions.
Published in the United States by Random House, Inc., New York, and
simultaneously in Canada by Random House of Canada Limited, Toronto.

Library of Congress Cataloging-in-Publication Data
Hirsch, Jay.
   More great American dream machines/Jay Hirsch.
      p. cm.
   ISBN 0-394-57532-6
   1. Antique and classic cars—United States.   I. Title.
TL23.H58 1990
   629.222'0973—dc20   90-53129

Manufactured in Italy
24689753

First Edition

Preface

DREAM MACHINE: an automobile that makes one's heart beat a little faster, stirs the imagination, brings a silly grin to the face, creates a slight sense of euphoria, and gets the juices flowing. A dream machine has style, soul, spirit—pizzazzz! Like a 1955 Studebaker President Speedster, 1957 Oldsmobile 98, or 1959 Plymouth Fury—all the cars that follow in this book.

Dream machines are not serious drivers' cars. Life is too short to be serious all the time. Dream machines are FUN. They are goin'-on-vacation-the-minute-you-get-behind-the-wheel cars. A dream machine is cloud-nine-not-a-care-in-the-world-ice-cream-baseball-apple-pie-summer-days-and-every-night-is-Saturday-night car!

There will be no judgments on the merit/beauty/garishness of some of these cars. They were designed by people who truly loved and enjoyed cars. They were designed for Americans . . . Americans who gave a helping hand to a good part of the world in a war called WW II. In a sense, the cars that follow were their reward for a job well done.

So sit back, pop a cold one, put a bib on if you think you might drool on the pictures, and maybe your dream machine will come rolling by.

Acknowledgments

I would like to thank all the wonderful people who let me photograph their cars, for their time and effort and the cold dinners they had to endure.

And Dan, may you awake one morning and have a purple monster staring you in the eye.

Contents

Contents

Appendixes

Introduction

Wow, oh boy, yee god, unreal, fantastic, oooh, ahh, unbelievable, allllright, luv ya car, great car, look at that interior, look at that backseat, look at THAT CAR!" These words and expressions are commonly heard by owners of dream machines. If you have not heard comments like these about your car, you are *not* driving a dream machine (no matter what the display ads for your car claim or what the salesperson who sold you the car told you).

"I like ya car." These four words were said when many of the cars in this book were new and are said all over again at car shows, drive-ins, shopping centers, and main streets from coast to coast—whenever they are seen.

No one says "I like your old car," but "I like your car!" The cars made in the golden (or chrome) age, the late 1940s through the early 1970s are not old; they are timeless American icons. The cars had names, names you could almost sink your teeth and soul into: Roadmaster, Crown Victoria, Skyliner, Impala, Mercury Turnpike Cruiser. The audacity of a company to actually call their car Turnpike Cruiser. With a name like that the car had better deliver both in style and performance, and deliver it did! "I'll be by to pick you up in my sun-yellow Turnpike Cruiser." Just the sound has such great expectations. A trip to the local Dairy Queen becomes an excursion, a travelogue of unknown wonders. "I'll be by to pick you up in my Probe." No thanks! Sounds like an unpleasant physical exam.

"Want to go for a spin in my Roadmaster?" Just the word itself—Roadmaster—and the mind is off onto some road to who knows where—or cares.

"I just got a Lexus, want to see it?" Noo way! Sounds like a skin disease.

The cars from this era not only had names, style, and spirit, but they had color: lavish two- and three-tone paint combinations in soft pastels and rich shades of blue, green, and red.

Hialeah green, sunburst yellow, Kimberly blue, emerald green, Persian sand, torch red, Thunderbird blue, Tahitian coral. The names themselves evoke a warm glow all over the minute you hear them. Not like Arctic white, a color to send shivers down one's spine. Give me a '57 Chevy Bel Air convertible in aqua any day or, better yet, on a warm summer night!

What is so special about these cars and their time? It was a time of peace and prosperity for the nation. By the time the mid-50s came around the memories of World War II and the Korean War were fading. It was time for the future and some fun. The country, the economy, the people, and especially the automobile industry responded.

What other country or people could make a 1950 Buick with its smiling grille or a 1953 Cadillac with those fabulous Dagmar bumpers? A 1955 Chevy has MADE IN THE U.S.A. stamped all over it waving the red, white, and blue—no matter what color the car is. Where else but in the U.S.A. could a car like the 1955 T-Bird be born? This is the "Fun, Fun, Fun," car that the Beach Boys sang about and every generation longs for.

There has never before or since been an automobile that has come to symbolize so much to so many people. In its purest form, the two-seat T-Bird was made from 1955 to 1957. Under 52,000 were produced, but the sensation it caused has never ceased. Thunderbird . . . the word is magic. A sporty, personal, fun car for just you and that someone special beside you—at a reasonable price. Thunderbird . . . nirvana right here on earth.

If the T-Bird was nirvana, then the Corvette is karma. GM introduced the car in 1954. It caused a stir but not the sensation GM hoped it would. The public didn't know how to perceive the car. For one thing it had plastic side curtains instead of roll-up glass windows. Side curtains went out in the 30s. The only other cars with side curtains were some odd European cars, which not only lacked roll-up windows but also adequate heaters and had the ride of a small pickup truck. The Corvette also had a fiberglass body—or just glass, as some people saw it.

If not for the T-Bird, GM would probably have discarded the Corvette. Because of the T-Bird—or in spite of it—GM stuck with the Corvette: company pride. In 1954, 3,400 Corvettes were built; in 1955, 700. In its first year the T-Bird sold 16,000.

The Corvette also had a straight 6-cylinder when first introduced, coupled with an automatic transmission. In 1955 a V-8 was added, and by 1957 one could have dual quads or fuel injection and "four on the floor" plus roll-up windows, which were introduced in 1956. Sales climbed to a little over 6,000 in 1957. The Corvette was on its way to becoming the best sports car in the world. That's right, the best in the world. There are some other cars which allude to being exotic, and they are, in the true meaning of the word: strange, outlandish, alien, not native to the place where found. The Corvette is all-American, and whether it has its famed 283, 350, or incredible 427 under the hood, there is certainly nothing strange or alien about it. Corvettes are on the road; exotics are usually in the shop.

The year 1955 not only saw the Thunderbird come forth but a dazzling array of new styling, colors, models (e.g., the four-door hardtop), and power options and safety conveniences for the car-buying public. It was the year Chevrolet received its first V-8, and a new look to put that V-8 in. The entire Chrysler lineup had the "Forward Look." The Imperial became a marque of its own, and the Chrysler 300 was born, the first true muscle car.

By 1957 there was not an option offered today (except for an AM/FM radio or computer) that you could not have on a 1957 model: from seat belts and shoulder harness to air-conditioning, power windows, tilt wheel, memory seat, air ride, automatic load leveling, torsion bar suspension, even Highway Hi-Fi (a specially constructed record player that had a shock-resistant arm which was offered in Chrysler products). There were also some items offered that you cannot buy today. The 1957 Lincoln had a self-lubrication system. The car had a separate canister for lube oil, and all one had to do was push a button and all the necessary parts of the car were lubricated—a true jiffy lube. The Lincoln also offered the limited-slip differential which "minimizes slippage on ice, even under hard braking." It could be had for the grand amount of $30!

1955 Thunderbird. Owner: Joe Patrissy/NY

Chrysler Corporation continued with its "Forward Look," but a new line was added—an ad line—"Suddenly It's 1960." During this golden era the car industry was always promising the future in their cars and car ads. This time period was and still is so popular that today many car ads show a "classic" from its past, and that past is almost always a 50s or 60s dream machine.

Chrysler's lineup was not only exhilarating to look at but the cars offered some features that were the future. Radios were transistorized. This may not seem like much today, but in 1957 when one turned on the nontransistorized car radio there was a warm-up period during which the tubes would actually get warm and then sound would come out of the speakers. There were also the previously mentioned Highway Hi-Fi, which Chrysler introduced in 1956. This was a special shock-resistant record player that spun a special seven-inch record disc. It took up about the same space as a box of tissues (which was also an option, with its own special under-dash dispenser), but by 1960 the highway hi-fi was no more. This listen-to-your-own-music idea was reborn in 1965 with eight-track stereo, which gave birth to cassettes and eventually CDs.

Oldsmobile and Pontiac offered the "sportable" radio. This was a transistorized radio that popped out of the dash to go with you on picnics or the beach. Today when one's radio is "popped out," it is not because it is a sportable; it either indicates a thief got it, or you have a removable unit that can be stored in your trunk so a thief won't get it.

During this period, fins were the rage through the entire Chrysler line, which only added to their low, long look. These cars were indeed low, ranging in height from fifty-four to fifty-seven inches. That is where the height of cars has remained to this day, except for some sporty cars, which are even lower.

The year 1957 was the final year for Hudson, a great car which, with its brute of a 6-cyl engine, was the stock-car champ from 1952 to 1954. Hudson got the auto industry rolling along into the "modern" era when in 1948 it brought out the step-down look. Until Hudson introduced this radical design, all cars were alike; you stepped up, into the car. The body of the car was above the chassis and side rails. All cars today are step-down cars. Take a look at the car you are driving: The floor is below the door sill. Hudson was the first car to do this.

The year also saw the end of Packard. By 1957, what was called a Packard was really a Studebaker with some minor trim changes. But what a car it was in its final days! In 1955, when Packard finally put their V-8 into production, it was just a little too late. Cadillac had a V-8 going back to 1916 and Lincoln had their V-12 and V-8 back in the 1930s. In 1952, when Lincoln went to an ohv V-8, it proved itself to the world in the famed Mexican Road Race three years straight (1952–1954).

The lucky few today who still have a 1955 or 1956 Packard know all too well what the world missed. This powerful 352 cid/ohv V-8 was run for ten days straight at the Proving Grounds in Utica, Michigan. The car averaged 104.737 mph for 10 days . . . 25,000 miles. The only time the car was stopped was to change drivers or to refuel.

And this was a luxury car, not some hard-riding, cold-in-the-winter, dusty-in-the-summer sports car. In addition, it had the most sophisticated suspension system of any car made, including today's. To go along with its unique torsion bar ride front and rear, the Packard had automatic load leveling. There was a small compressor in the trunk that was run by an electric motor that "sensed" when additional weight was added to the car or taken away, always keeping the car on an even keel no matter what the weight of the passenger or luggage load.

Ford was not sitting on the sidelines while GM and Chrysler were at work. In addition to their T-Bird, Ford had some ideas which came to light in 1957 and 1958. In 1957 Ford brought forth to the world the convertible of convertibles—the Skyliner. This was a true hardtop (as in all-steel top) convertible. At the push of a button the driver started in motion a group of motors and electrical wiring which raised the trunk lid backward, lifted the metal top, and lowered it back into the trunk. When this entire operation was completed, in about thirty seconds, there was one clean sweep of dream machine with no telltale ugly boot to signal where the top was stored. The car was made until 1959. Ford felt that sales of 48,000 over three years were not enough to continue this unique car.

On Mercury's top-of-the-line model, the Turnpike Cruiser, the rear window was electrically controlled by the driver (and the driver only) and it could be lowered for ventilation or all the way down for cooling. This was in addition to the Cruiser's quad headlights, twin air intake units above the front windshield, memory seat, 368 cid V-8, and full cruiser fender skirts.

The other idea Ford had was the Edsel, the year—1958. Ford produced 63,000 cars, but sales of 200,000 were expected of this overpromoted, overresearched, underbacked-up-by-the-Ford-Motor-Company car. Plans were being made before model year 1959 for the demise of the Edsel. The same year was also a recession year for the country, and car sales suffered among the Big Three.

American Motors under the leadership of George Romney turned out 162,000 Ramblers in 1958. At the same time the Japan Automobile Industry Association in Tokyo announced plans (to no one's interest) to ship 1,500 cars to the United States.

In addition to the Rambler, American Motors had the Metropolitan, a cute English-built car that delivered 35+ mpg. There was also an assortment of foreign cars, all European. There was Austin, MG, Triumph, Alfa Romeo, Fiat, Renault Dauphine (with a rear-mounted water-cooled engine), Opel, Vauxhall, Jaguar, Goggomobile, Mercedes, Simca, Porsche, Sunbeam, and a funny-looking German car called Volkswagen, which sold over 200,000 cars in 1958. The model was fondly called the Beetle.

If the automobile was starting to bring uniformity to many aspects of American life, Americans compensated by requiring diversity in their cars. Small segments of the market were carving out little niches for themselves whether they knew it or not. The station wagon was gaining in popularity as a true automobile, not just a utility vehicle; convertibles were fun; sports cars were "macho"—or foolish if you happened to care about keeping warm and dry with healthy kidneys! Just as there was status in the multicolored chrome machines, a reverse snobbishness was developing over foreign cars.

For the ultimate connoisseur of individuality there were the customs/leadsleds/hot rods/jalopies. A jalopy was an old car that was as dilapidated as possible. Its ability to function at all was deemed a miracle by most who would see it. But even jalopies tugged at a person's heart and after a while these were often "fixed up." But being old (usually from the late 1940s and older), many sheet metal and trim parts were hard to find. Since these cars were truly for the free-spirited, why not go one step further and make a statement? Many jalopies had their body lines reworked, grille work was removed (as was chrome in many cases), sometimes the car was lowered, and finally an outlandish paint job was applied. Leadsleds/customs were the result. A 1934 "Purple Monster" Ford Coupe (see pages 115–17) is a true 50s (and today) dream machine.

Taking a conventional engine, reboring cylinders, and installing extra carburetors and special cams to boost power produced the so-called hot rod. The auto industry caught up with this trend in the mid-60s with the Pontiac GTO, Dodge Challenger, Ford Shelby Cobra, and Plymouth Superbird. Performance? The 1964 GTO went from 0–60 in 5.7 seconds and was capable of 135+ mph, with an engine you could actually work on without a degree in computer science!

By the late 60s some people in the auto industry seemed to be keeping their heads too close to the exhaust for they came up with the air spoiler. The spoiler was to muscle cars as the fin was to cars of the 50s. Again Chrysler Corporation had to go one better and the result was the Superbird. Even GM knew when enough was enough and did not try to outdo this one.

Fins, chrome, windows that went all the way up and down on both the front and rear doors and with no pillars to obstruct your view: the hardtop. Putting all the windows down on a warm summer day, going for a ride in the country and smelling the grass, trees, the outdoors; radios with knobs and buttons big enough to see and put your finger on, not the size of a baby's pinky finger . . . that's a dream machine.

Pink, pastel green, turquoise, Pompeiian red; blue jeans, white T-shirts, sneakers; *Rebel Without a Cause*, *The Wild One*, rock 'n' roll, and Elvis Presley. The movie *Rebel Without a Cause* featured a young actor by the name of James Dean. He drove a 1950 Mercury, wore a white T-shirt and blue jeans, and shed a tear when a friend died. In *The Wild One*, another young actor named Marlon Brando wore a black leather motorcycle jacket, a cloth biker's hat, jeans, and a white T-shirt. Rock 'n' roll and Elvis are one. No other country could turn out the cars of the 50s and 60s or produce such heros as James Dean, Marlon, and Elvis.

Civic and church leaders alike preached that these newfound celebrities and this new music would be the downfall of the United States. The playing of rock 'n' roll and the wearing of blue jeans and leather jackets was banned in many communities.

Today jeans, leather jackets, and sneakers are fashion the world over. Rock 'n' roll—some of it may be frivolous, but the message is freedom and fun, just as in a good pair of Levi's. For a time in the late 70s some people were turning out "designer jeans," even French designer jeans. The audacity to imply that Levi's needed improvement! That's like saying you've made a better '55 Thunderbird, or have an improved '57 Ford or Chevy. No way; the best has been achieved, leave well enough alone.

Pink Cadillac. That is what happens when you take one of your favorite colors and combine it with your favorite car. Elvis had a fondness for Cadillacs and Lincolns, and his favorite colors were pink, black, and charcoal gray. Put it all together and you have a '56 pink Coupe de Ville. Could you imagine a pink Mercedes, Honda, Rolls-Royce, or Toyota? Why, Toyotas don't even have white-

1957 Chevrolet Bel Air. Owner: Steve Herson/NY

walls. Any of these cars in pink would be absurd. But on a Cadillac it's outrageous, it's ostentatious, it's great. The only thing outrageous about a BMW, Mercedes, or Lexus is its price. Now *that's* ostentatious.

The golden age of cars and the music that was born then represent freedom, the free spirit in each individual. "People everywhere just wanna be free," sung by the Rascals, a rock group of the 60s, sums it up. From Moscow to Miami all young people know "the Boss" (Bruce Springsteen)—and what a 1957 Chevy is. When people are listening to the same song, dancing to the same music and that music is coming over their radio of their '57 Ford or Chevy, even if it is only in their dreams, you have a friend.

A friend at a car show said to me recently, "Ever notice how when someone is hungry they usually say they could eat a cow—you know they want a nice big, juicy steak. People have a cookout or clambake and they mean food, real food: beef, burgers, steamed clams, lobster, cold beer (and not that wimpy light stuff either). You never hear someone say, 'Wow, I could go for some salmon mousse, or a real nice goose pâté, or chicken in an herb-cream sauce.' "

Another friend went on, "Yeah, it's like you go to someone's house and they show you a painting, and this person says, 'It's a _Chagallso._' Look, I may not know much about paintings, but I know when I don't like something, and most people are the same. Ride down the street in a '57 Ford convertible, '59 Caddy, or '63 split-window 'Vette, and people say, 'WOW, look at that car,' even if they don't know what kind of car it is or how much it is worth. These American cars from the 50s are sculpture, art, icons . . . yeah, a '49 custom Mercury in candy-apple red . . . is that American or not?"

A friend who is a doctor and also happens to own a 1955 cruiser has done some casual scientific/medical research into the human mind and social behavior at car shows and how people react around dream machines. "It is a primeval reaction at first. A person starts uttering sounds: oooh, ah, yay, yee. Then sounds that are the beginning of simple words come out: wow, oh boy, yeah, which progress to simple words and phrases: great, fantastic, unbelieveable, I like your car, what year is it? The facial muscles are very relaxed, the body loose, and there is oftentimes a huge smile or grin. The person is bordering on a state of euphoria. After babbling on for several minutes, it seems the mind is able to compose itself and regroup, so to speak. The individual starts to talk in more complex sentences, but still with a big grin and much animation. They are fine until their next encounter with a '59 Caddy or '60 Lincoln and the process starts all over. This is really fantastic, medically speaking. It is a proven fact that just keeping a person in a laughing, smiling, I-feel-good-all-over state of mind is very healthy."

Next time you see someone driving a '50 Buick or '59 Plymouth or whatever chrome-age car, take a good look at that person. Odds are they are smiling. Their hands are gently holding the steering wheel. Maybe the left elbow is resting on the door frame with the window down. This is not as foolish or dangerous as it may appear. Because of the height of the seat and the size of the steering wheel in relation to the top half of the door, a driver can have his elbow on the door edge (with the window down) and still have his left hand on the steering wheel along with his right hand.

Ever see someone behind the wheel of a BMW or Acura? Often it's a white-knuckles-on-the-wheel, eyes-bulging, get-right-on-your-bumper, blow-the-horn, outa-my-way look—a look of total constipation. Get a Mustang, a people-friendly car. Get rid of that "technologically advanced, computer-designed, wind-tunnel, refined, never-touched-by-a-Raymond-Loewy-type-mind, can't-lower-the-rear-side-windows, coefficient-drag machine. Drive a car that smiles at you with a big how-are-you grin.

This was an era when people bought cars for the sheer joy of buying a new car, and they didn't have to mortgage the house to do it. People actually went to new car dealers with the same enthusiasm as when going to the World Series or to see their favorite college football team in a bowl game. It was late September or early October, the World Series was underway and "the new cars arrived." It was fall and dealer showrooms looked like Broadway on opening night; there was electricity in the air!

Today that excitement lives on in the many car shows held around the United States from April to October ever year—especially October, when the air becomes a little crisper, the leaves start to change color, and the days become a little shorter. To many people the world over October means just one word—HERSHEY, as in Hershey, Pennsylvania, and the Antique Car Club of America's fall meet.

Every autumn since 1954, when seven vendors and slightly over 200 cars were on display at Hershey Estates, people have been coming to Hershey in the fall. For three days (either the first or second weekend in October) what was once a local event has grown into what has become the Woodstock of car shows. If you remember Woodstock or have seen the film, that is Hershey—but every year and with proper toilet facilities and lodging. From sunrise to sunset people make their way among 9,000 vendor spaces to find parts for anything from a 1903 Oldsmobile to a 1963 Corvette. On Saturday, which is show day, over 2,000 cars are on display, the newest being twenty-five years old. Hershey is where a wife grabs her husband to go look "at this fantastic 1936 Ford roadster," and the car she grabbed him out of is their 1935 Duesenberg. This is where 200,000 headlight-eyed, piston-brained, oil-in-their-veins car nuts come to look, swap, dream, and buy car parts and cars. Hershey is the world's largest Toys Я Us Store . . . the only difference between men and boys is the price of their toys.

On any warm summer night or sunny weekend afternoon from New York to California, from Surf Avenue to Sunset Boulevard to Rt. 66 to Main Street in Altus, OK, there are forty-five-year-old teens in their '59 Caddys waving to nineteen-year-old teens in their '57 Chevys and just as they pass each other there is a ten-year-old on the side of the road pulling at his father's arm, shouting, "Wow, Dad, look at that car!"

A Word About Submarine Races (Submarine Race Watching)

A unique phenomenon of the mid-1950s was submarine race watching. It is generally credited to a New York City disc jockey by the name of Murray Kaufman ("Murray the K"), with the cooperation of the Coast Guard and the help of the U.S. Navy.

After World War II the navy mothballed most of the battleships, cruisers, and submarines that had been in use during the war. Conventionally powered submarines in particular fell on hard times in the 50s with the emergence of the nuclear sub fathered by Admiral Hyman Rickover.

Murray Kaufman had a brilliant idea: Why not create some inexpensive, safe entertainment for young people and those young at heart and also some training for the navy by having submarines race on the East and Hudson rivers surrounding Manhattan island? The Coast Guard found no problem with the plan except that for commercial shipping purposes both waterways could not be used on the same night. It was agreed to use the East River on Friday nights and the Hudson on Saturday nights.

In a very short time this grew to be an immensely popular spectator sport. On Saturday nights especially, cars would line the New Jersey Palisades and stay most of the night to get a good view of the submarines. Even in lousy weather the races would go on; since they were underwater the weather had no adverse effect on the outcome.

The sport gained new supporters each week. People started to come not only on weekends but on weeknights too. They would choose a spot they thought would offer a good view for Friday or Saturday or just park and think of the previous weekend's event.

Word of this event spread across the country. Soon radio stations and municipalities from coast to coast were sending inquiries to the Coast Guard and Murray the K as to how to go about organizing these races. Some smaller cities, especially inland, wanted to know how a submarine could be transported to their locale.

Finally, a joint statement was released by the Coast Guard and Murray the K. Its essence was: The main element in this exhilarating sporting event is the spectators. In fact, it has been discovered that you do not even need submarines or water either—just a decent stretch of land and a car with a plush interior.

More
Great American
Dream
Machines

1941 *Packard Darrin*/180

To start the new decade (the 40s) Packard Motors hired Howard "Dutch" Darrin to design their new models, including a special upscale model, perhaps in anticipation of Edsel Ford's Lincoln Continental.

Dutch Darrin—the name sounds like a middle linebacker for the Chicago Bears. But Dutch was anything but. He was a designer, a car designer. From 1922 until 1937 he lived in Paris and was a custom coach builder for Minerva, a prestigious Belgian automaker.

Upon Darrin's return to the United States in 1937, he opened a custom design studio in Hollywood, California. Except for the Cord 810, Dutch held most other American car designs in contempt. He was a flamboyant

Specifications

Overall Length	215½"
Width	76⅛"
Height	64"
Weight*	3,920 lbs
Wheelbase	127"
Engine	L-head straight 8-cyl 356 cid (cubic inch displacement)/5.8 liter
Carburetor	2 bbls (barrels)
Horsepower**	165 @ 3,600 rpm
Bore & Stroke	3.50 x 4.625
Compression Ratio	6.85:1
Electrical	6 volt
Fuel Tank	20 gals
Cooling System	20 qts
Tires	7.00 x 15
Suspension	front: coil springs rear: leaf springs
Frame	X-member, box section, side rails
Transmission	3-speed/manual overdrive (optional)
Rear Axle Ratio	3.92:1
Price***	$4,783
Owner	Vintage Car Store/NY

Accessories

Heater/Defroster (Optional)
Radio (Optional)
Trip Odometer
Fuel, Amps, Temperature, and Oil Gauges (Standard)
Directional Signals (Standard)
Rear Fender Skirts (Optional)
Goddess of Speed Hood Ornament (Optional)
Cormorant Hood Ornament (Optional)

*Shipping weight
**Brake horsepower (BHP)
***Less accessories (options)

character, and so were most of the film stars and movie studio heads who became his clientele. These people had money, and money was one of the prime raw materials in custom coach building.

In 1939 when Packard was looking for a new styling statement they turned to Dutch. Dutch is credited with the basic design of the 1941 Packard Clipper (no running boards) and his masterpiece, the Packard Darrin/180. (In the early 50s Dutch would collaborate with Kaiser, the result being the Kaiser Darrin.)

The Packard Darrin was the past and future, elegant and sporty. It retained a small running board, but was also low and streamlined for the period. The side dip in the door created an illusion that the car was lower and longer that it actually was. (Running boards, those long steplike platforms on the sides of all cars, started to be phased out in 1940. Except for the 1936 Cord, cars would have running boards until 1941.)

The Packard Darrin was sold through Packard dealers with a price of $4,783. A 1940 Ford sold for about $900. The car was a success, especially for a custom-bodied car. Dutch could not meet demand in his custom studio in Hollywood, and so he moved operations to the closed-down Auburn plant in Connersville, Ohio. In 1941 he moved to a plant in Cincinnati, Ohio.

On December 7, 1941, Pearl Harbor was attacked by the Japanese, which brought the United States into World War II. Packard entered into wartime production of engines for PT boats and airplanes, and Dutch Darrin was out of the design business for Packard.

In today's auto market with each manufacturer dishing out superlatives about their cars, one of the most often used words is "performance." In the true meaning of the word—something accomplished—the Packard Darrin leaves them all eating dust!

1947 *Lincoln Continental Cabriolet*

Edsel Ford, the son of Henry Ford, who founded the Ford Motor Company, was president of the Lincoln division in the 1920s and 1930s. Henry Ford bought Lincoln from Henry Martyn Leland in 1922 for $8,000,000 at the urging of his son Edsel—and also to give Edsel something to do. Henry was a tyrant, not only as a captain of industry, but as a father and person as well. He wanted to sell cars for transportation and in any color of black the public wanted. Edsel thought people wanted more in a car and that Ford should have a flagship for its company. To appease Edsel, Henry bought Lincoln.

H. M. Leland had also founded another luxury automobile at the beginning of the century which eventually became part of the GM stable, the Cadillac.

Edsel Ford was a frequent traveler to Europe, or the Continent as it was referred to by the wealthy Americans who took the ocean liners in the 1930s (there were no jets, yet alone prop planes crossing the Atlantic then).

On one of Edsel's trips to Europe he brought back an English sports car. Edsel showed this continental car to a young Ford designer by the name of Eugene T. Gregorie. Edsel asked E.T. why Lincoln couldn't make a personal type sporty car. So E.T. started sketching and designing a personal type car for Edsel Ford. He knew if he had this project designated as anything other than personal, Henry Ford would kill it.

At first Gregorie tried to work with some Ford chassis, but he could not get the long sweeping fender effect he wanted from them. Ed Martin, another employee in the Ford design department, suggested to Gregorie and Edsel that they try the new Lincoln Zephyr chassis and the Zephyr convertible as a model to begin with. What followed was a true 1950s leadsled. The entire car had four inches taken out of it horizontally (sectioning) and was then welded back together. The windshield glass was cut and squared off, and the car was lowered. All this work was done by hand.

The car was completed in late 1938 and was sent to Palm Beach, Florida, where Edsel spent his winter vacation. It attracted immediate and glorious attention from Edsel's friends and in a short time he had 200 firm orders.

Upon the car's return to the Lincoln plant in 1939, plans and work were begun to manufacture the car now known as "the Continental" (as it was referred to in Palm Beach). The spare tire mounted on the rear was for a European look. The terms "Continental kit" or "Continen-

Specifications

Overall Length	217"
Width	front/75.68" rear/72.82"
Height	63"
Weight	4,135 lbs
Wheelbase	125"
Engine**	flat-head/V-12/292 cid/4.8 liter
Carburetor	2 bbls
Horsepower	125 @ 4,000 rpm
Bore & Stroke	2.875 x 3.75
Compression Ratio	7.20:1
Electrical	6 volt
Fuel Tank	19.5 gals
Cooling System	24½ qts
Tires	8.20 x 15
Suspension	front: transverse spring
	rear: transverse spring
Frame	X-type
Transmission	3-speed manual with overdrive
Rear Axle Ratio	4.22:1
Price	$4,800
Owner	George M. Edwards/NJ

**For model year 1942 Lincoln used a 305 cid/V-12. In 1947 and 1948 Lincoln returned to the original 292 cid/V-12. 1948 was the last year of the Continental and of a V-12 engine in the United States.

tal tire" became popular in the 50s. The name "Continental" referred to the car, not the tire. The first 54 Cabriolets (as the convertibles were called) and 350 club coupes were produced for 1940. They had the Lincoln Zephyr 292 cid V-12, and door handles. In 1941 buttons would replace the door handles, through the last year of production in 1948. The first year of production, 1940, the car did not carry the Continental name; it was added on in 1941.

In 1942 the Continental got a minor face lift and also a slightly larger version of the V-12. It was now 305 cid. In 1947 the car would again have the 292. The front end was restyled again for 1947 and that result is seen here.

The purpose of the V-12 was not for sheer off-the-line performance but smoothness and quiet. The more cylinders a car has, the smoother and quieter the engine will be and with less vibration to the chassis or body.

As a test on your new car, try taking a five-minute time exposure of the car with the motor running. When you get the prints back see if there is a slight blur to the picture (there will be). The rearview photo of the Continental with the brake light on (by the license plate frame) was a five-minute exposure with the car running. About the brake light: It was standard on the Continental and some other cars of the 30s and 40s.

Some people did not understand the real purpose of the V-12 and were disappointed in its lackluster off-the-line pickup. But on the highway or open road the car could cruise at 90 mph for hours on end while delivering 17–20 mpg.

The car you see here is exceptional for many reasons. It is a convertible, and the color, the scarlet interior, and the condition of the car are superb. But what really makes it unique is the owner, George Edwards. George bought the car in 1947; he is the only owner/master this

Accessories

Power Windows
Power Seat
Whitewall Tires
Heater/Defroster
Radio
Leather Interior
Power Antenna
Fuel, Oil, Amps, and Temperature Gauges
Electric Clock
Trip Odometer
Power Convertible Top
Directional Signals

car has ever known (though at times some of George's friends question who owns who).

Take a good long look at the interior of this Continental. No Ph.D. from MIT with a degree in ergonomics designed those leather seats. A computer with all its powers could never devise a color or interior that complement each other so well.

A craftsman with many years experience custom made and fitted that interior. Human hands shaped and molded the steel that is used for the body from a design that came out of a person with an inner spirit. Here is an automobile that was designed to arouse one's senses, to move you even before you entered the car.

The car was offered in two body styles only, the Cabriolet (convertible) and Club Coupe (hardtop). Since the cars were virtually handmade, no two front fenders are exactly alike—which was no small problem when it came to repairing or replacing a fender or door.

In an early ad for the Continental in 1940 a closing line goes, "more fun per gallon." At almost $3,500 in 1940, that was a lot for fun.

In a special exhibition by the Museum of Modern Art in New York City in 1951 the Continental was chosen for its "excellence in styling.... The Continental satisfies the requirements of connoisseurs while capturing the imagination of a public less preoccupied with the refinements of automobile design." In other words, it looks great!

1949 *Mercury Station Wagon* (Woody)

The 1949 Mercury seen here is a slightly modified or custom woody. The front parking lights, hood emblem, and grille are from a 1950 Mercury. The vinyl roof is not an original item, although it was available in 1950 on the two-door Monterey coupe. The Mercury of 1948,

9

Specifications

Overall Length	213.88"
Width	76.8"
Height	70"
Weight	3,750 lbs
Wheelbase	118"
Engine	L-head/V-8/225.4 cid/3.7 liter
Carburetor	2 bbls
Horsepower	110 @ 3,600 rpm
Bore & Stroke	3.19 x 4
Compression Ratio	6.8:1
Electrical	6 volt
Fuel Tank	19½ gals
Cooling System	22 qts/pressure type, 2 water pumps
Tires	7.10 x 15
Suspension	front: independent, coil springs rear: solid axle, leaf springs
Frame	double-drop X-type
Transmission	3-speed manual overdrive (optional)
Rear Axle Ratio	4.27:1
Price	$2,600
Owner	Charles Edwards/NJ

Accessories

Radio
Heater/Defroster
Power Windows (Standard on Convertible)
Padded Canvas or Vinyl Roof (Standard on Monterey Coupe)
Spotlights
Leather Interior
Whitewall Tires
Power Seat

the last year of the pre-World War II body style, also had a vinyl roof. These were four-door woody wagons which still had the wood frame for a top. The tailgate-mounted spare should be metal enclosed, not vinyl encased as on this car. Aside from these minor "infractions," the car looks great and is original. The owner just fixed it up his way.

The Mercury woodys of 1949 to 1951 were only offered in two-door versions (same with Ford). In 1952 the wagon became a four-door with wood trim along the side of the car. The two-door would be an all-steel body with no character!

1950 *Plymouth (P-20) Station Wagon (Woody)*

The top of the line for Plymouth in 1950 was their woody wagon. At $2,600 it was $300 more than a convertible and $800 more than a Plymouth four-door sedan. Wood and automobiles have always created a certain mystery and beauty. Chrysler had the Town & Country convertibles in the late 1940s; Rolls-Royce made some all-wood boattails in the 1930s; and until 1953 most American-made wagons had some wood trim. Today's

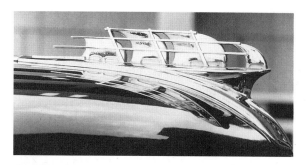

Specifications

Overall Length	192⅝"
Width	73⅝"
Height	67½"
Weight	3,353 lbs
Wheelbase	118½"
Engine	L-head/6-cyl/217.7 cid/3.6 liter
Carburetor	1 bbl
Horsepower	97 @ 3,600 rpm
Bore & Stroke	3.25 x 4.375
Compression Ratio	7.0:1
Electrical	6 volt
Fuel Tank	17 gals
Cooling System	16½ qts
Tires	6.70 x 15
Suspension	front: independent, coil springs
	rear: solid axle, leaf springs
Frame	box
Transmission	3-speed manual
Rear Axle Ratio	4.1:1
Price	$2,600
Owner	Ernest Fodor/NJ

Accessories

Radio
Heater/Defroster
Whitewall Tires
Electric Clock
External Sunshade for Front Window
Rear Fender Chrome Gravel Guards
Fog Lamps
Outside Rearview Mirror
Spotlight
Directional Signals
Leather Interior

wagons offer a "simulated wood-grain look" as an option.

The original woodys were produced in the 1930s. Their entire rear upper bodies were made of wood, either ash or oak. The roof was a wood frame with vinyl fabric laid across it to prevent rain from coming in through the cracks. After World War II the woodys had a steel top with wood sides and doors. The woodys that GM and Ford made from 1951 to 1953 had exterior wood trim only.

The 1950 Plymouth woody was the last Chrysler Corporation woody (DeSoto and Chrysler offered woodys the same year). The blending of wood, chrome and painted metal give the car a character that remains impressive to this day.

Sitting inside one of these "panelled dens on wheels" with its leather interior is pure delight. (In the 1930s before the steel roof you would be looking up at a headliner of wood beams.)

The problem of what to do with the spare in wagons is solved gracefully: the lower half of the tailgate is slightly wider with a cutout, and there is a locking cover over the spare. Simple and effective.

1950 *Ford Station Wagon (Woody)*

Surf's up! If ever there was the archetypal woody wagon, it is Ford's from 1949 to 1951. The only difference between the years was that in 1951 there would be two spinners in the front grille.

13

Specifications

Overall Length	208″
Width	73″
Height	68″
Weight	3,511 lbs
Wheelbase	114″
Engine	flat-head/V-8/239 cid/3.9 liter
Carburetor	2 bbls
Horsepower	100 @ 3,600 rpm
Bore & Stroke	3.19 x 3.75
Compression Ratio	6.8:1
Electrical	6 volt
Fuel Tank	19 gals
Cooling System	22 qts
Tires	7.10 x 15
Suspension	front: independent, coil springs rear: solid axle, variable ratio springs
Frame	double-drop X-type
Transmission	3-speed manual overdrive (optional)
Rear Axle Ratio	4.27:1
Price	$2,028
Owner	Melvyn Lipschitz/NY

Accessories

Radio
Heater/Defroster
Directional Signals
Whitewall Tires
Sunshade for Front Window
Spotlight
Brake Light (on station wagons, only one light was required by law; the passenger side brake light was an option)

These wagons have probably carried more surfboards than any other vehicle made. As cheap, roomy transportation, they introduced a whole new generation to a simple and fun form of getting around.

As any item that has "endured," these cars have gone from beach woodys to valuable collectors' cars today. Sure, many are still used for fun; that is what all cars are meant for. Just be careful how you lay that board down in there!

After 1951, Ford would no longer make the woody wagon in a two-door, or separate, body style. After 1953 the wood would be "simulated." That is like imitation crab legs: It serves a purpose, but it's nothing like the real thing.

1950 *Studebaker Commander Land Cruiser*

I n 1947 Studebaker came out with their new postwar look. General Motors, Ford, and Chrysler would not come out with their new design look until 1949. Studebaker knew that it needed to freshen up its

15

Specifications

Overall Length	197½"
Width	69⅞"
Height	61½"
Weight	3,265 lbs
Wheelbase	120"
Engine	L-head/6-cyl/245.6 cid/4.0 liter
Carburetor	1 bbl
Horsepower	102 @ 3,200 rpm
Bore & Stroke	3.312 x 4.75
Compression Ratio	7.0:1
Electrical	6 volt
Fuel Tank	18 gals
Cooling System	10 qts
Tires	6.70 x 15
Suspension	front: independents, coil springs
	rear: solid axle, leaf springs
Frame	ladder
Transmission	3-speed manual with Hill Holder
Rear Axle Ratio	4.10:1
Price	$2,024
Owner	Stan Rudoff/NY

Accessories

Hill Holder
Directional Signals
Whitewall Tires
Radio 8-Tube Push-button
      6-Tube Push-button
      6-Tube Manual
Antenna (Vacuum Power/Front Fender or Reel-Controlled Cowl Type)
Heater/Defroster
Rear Fender Skirts
Exterior Windshield Sun Visor (Front Window)
Grease Fitting Lubri Caps
Locking Gas Cap
Backup Lights
Fog Lights
Spotlight
Parking Brake Warning Light
Under-Hood Light
Trunk Light
Tissue Dispenser
Windshield Washer
Venetian Blinds (Rear Window)
Custom Luggage

Vanity Mirror
Battery Vitalizer
Frame Oil Filter (Standard on Commander)

styling by 1950 and thus was born the "bullet nose," or which-is-the-front-and-which-is-the-rear look.

By midyear Studebaker was even offering a propeller option that attached to the bullet nose. When the car was moving the propeller, which was driven by the wind, created the look of a grounded helicopter with the wrong propeller or a nerd's beanie.

The bullet nose was made for 1950 and 1951. In 1952 a more traditional front was put on, and in 1953 a revolution in design emerged in the form of the Raymond Loewy–styled Studebaker. These cars were low, sleek, and had a timeless beauty that still looks good today—and which can also be seen in the 1955 President Speedster (see pages 37–38).

The 1950 bullet nose seen here has been in the same family since new. It has recently undergone a cosmetic face lift, stripped to bare metal and repainted, front and rear bumpers rechromed, and original material seat covers replaced. But the power plant/drive train—the motor and transmission—have never been touched except for normal maintenance.

Imagine waking each morning and being greeted by a bullet-nose Commander! That look seems to be saying, "We're going to have fun today!" The name Commander—you just want to go anywhere in a car with that name. Not like Camry, which sounds like something ominous that is breaking down the ozone layer.

"My Land Crusier is waiting for me . . ."

1950 Buick Roadmaster

It greets you each morning." That was a headline on an ad for a 1950 Buick. Look at that grille, the most famous of all Buick grilles. If ever a car flashed its ivories or chrome, this is it. Here is a Pepsodent smile to end all Pepsodent smiles.

Imagine starting each day with this car and that grille eagerly awaiting to greet you! Upon entering, those high club-chair seats just wait to cradle your body. Just sitting in this car is a vacation. This is a Buick Roadmaster. The audacity of a company to call their car Roadmaster!

Specifications

Overall Length	208.8″
Width	80″
Height	64.4″
Weight	4,345 lbs
Wheelbase	126¼″
Engine	OHV straight 8-cyl/320 cid/5.2 liter
Carburetor	2 bbls
Horsepower	152 @ 3,600 rpm
Bore & Stroke	3.437 x 4.312
Compression Ratio	6.9:1
Electrical	6 volt
Fuel Tank	19 gals
Cooling System	19 qts
Tires	8.20 x 15
Suspension	front: independent, coil springs rear: solid axle, coil springs
Frame	high carbon pressed steel X-type
Transmission	automatic (Dynaflow)
Rear Axle Ratio	3.6:1
Price	$3,050
Owner	Georgette & Bill Braga/NJ

Accessories

Heater/Defroster (Standard)
Power Seat
Outside Mirror (Driver's Side and Passenger Side)
Power Windows
Electric Clock
Power Top
Leather Interior
Trip Odometer
Radio (Standard)
Fuel and Temperature Gauges
Full-Size Spare Tire
Outside Mirror with Spotlight
Color: Royal Maroon Metallic with Matching Leather Interior

But this car lives up to that name and then some. Five-mph bumpers? Why, bricks crumble at the sight of this Roadmaster!

The car you see here has undergone a complete restoration by Bill and Georgette Braga, not by a restoration shop. The car was taken down to bare metal, fenders and doors removed, new wiring harnesses installed, minor mechanical work done to the engine (which is in great shape), chassis cleaned, new carpet and leather interior, and new canvas top installed. Except for the replating of the chrome, Bill and Georgette did everything in the garage by their house.

One of the most important tools that Bill used was patience. I point this out to the novice who is afraid to buy an old car, let alone do any work on it. Bill is no genius (and many of his friends are quick to agree), just a guy with pride, common sense, and a brain who knows how to think and reason.

Bill and Georgette think of 1,000 mile trips as a cruise. If you were curious about the kind of work that Bill did on the car: whenever it is displayed at car shows, it always takes a first, rarely a second. The paint, which is 90 percent of what the eye sees, is flawless. What you don't see, unless you get down or look under the hood, is equally flawless.

Next time you are fortunate enough to see a Buick of this era, take a good look at the owner and his smile; it usually mirrors the grille.

1950 *Hudson Pacemaker*
1951 *Hudson Commodore*

Founded in 1909 by Roy D. Chapin with the financial backing of J. L. Hudson of the Hudson department store and later chain (both now defunct), Hudson produced cars in the medium-price range that were really high-price caliber.

After World War II while other automakers were still panning off prewar designs to the car-hungry public, Hudson introduced the "step-down," or torpedo, look in 1948. It was a unit body-type car and was lower than the previous model and any other car then on the market by almost six inches.

The floor pan was dropped between the chassis side rails. This put the floor lower than the door sills—common practice today, but very radical in 1948. The car had a smooth, slablike side, and with the optional skirts and sloping back, the nickname "torpedo back" was at times applied to the car. It was considered "aerodynamic" for its day.

In the sedan, the center armrest in the rear was eighteen inches wide, more like a small end table in a living room suspended between two club chairs. The dropping of the floor pan not only resulted in a lower, sleeker car, but also a lower center of gravity. The car handled and cornered well, to say the least.

In 1951 the 308 cid inline 6-cyl was offered in the Hornet series. It had "twin-H," or 2-1 bbl carburetors. From 1952 to 1954 Hudsons dominated the NASCAR race circuit. In 1953 Marshall Teague won twelve of thirteen AAA stock car events in a Hudson. With drivers such as Frank Mundy and Dick Rathmann behind the wheel, Hornets won sixty-five NASCAR victories between 1952 and 1954, a record that still stands today.

Opposite: 1951 Hudson Commodore (foreground); 1950 Hudson Pacemaker

Pacemaker
Specifications

Overall Length	201½"
Width	77¹/₁₆"
Height	60⅜"
Weight	3,600 lbs
Wheelbase	119"
Engine	L-head/6-cyl/232 cid/3.8 liter
Carburetor	1 bbl
Horsepower	112 @ 4,000 rpm
Bore & Stroke	3.56 x 3.875
Compression Ratio	7.2:1
Electrical	6 volt
Fuel Tank	20 gals
Cooling System	19½ qts
Tires	7.60 x 15
Suspension	front: ind, coil springs
	rear: solid axle, leaf springs
Frame	mono body
Transmission	3-speed with overdrive (optional)
	Super-Matic (optional)
Rear Axle Ratio	4.1:1
Price	$3,100
Owner	Dick and Dee Hitt/NJ

Accessories

Backup Light
Battery Filler (Automatic)
Cigar Lighter
Clock (Manual Windup) Electric Clock (Optional)
Directional Signals
Emergency Trouble Light
Exhaust Deflector
Fire Extinguisher
Fog Lamps
Hubcap Kit (Large)
Hydraulic Jack
Tissue Dispenser
Mirror (Outside Driver's Side; Vanity Mirror,
Passenger Side; Sun Visor)
Oil Filter
Radiator Grille Guard
Radio
Rear Bumper Guard
Spare Tire Valve Extension
Spotlight
Steering Wheel Kit (18")
Trunk Light
Under-Hood Light
Windshield Washer
Leather Interior (Standard on Convertible)
Power Windows (Hydraulic, Standard on Convertible)
Convertible Top colors (Tan, Black, or Maroon Canvas)
Fender Skirts

By 1951 all the car manufacturers had finally come out with their new postwar designs. The Hudson look was now three years old. Being a unit body, it was not easy and cheap to bring out a new body style. By 1953 sales were slumping, even though the Hornet was eating up the competition on the stock car circuit.

The 1954 Hudson merged with Nash. For the model year 1955 the Hudson was more of a restyled Nash than a Hudson. Model year 1957 would see the end of the Hudson nameplate.

Commodore
Specifications

Overall Length	208″
Width	77⅝″
Height	60⅜″
Weight	3,620 lbs
Wheelbase	124″
Engine	L-head 8-cyl/254 cid/4.2 liter
	L-head 6-cyl/308 cid/5.0 liter
	(Hornet)
Carburetor	2 bbls/Commodore 2-1 bbl/Hornet
Horsepower	128 @ 4,200 rpm (254)
	145 @ 3,800 rpm (308)
Bore & Stroke	3 x 4.50/254 cid
	3.81 x 4.50/308 cid
Compression Ratio	7.1:1 (same for Hornet)
Electrical	6 volt
Fuel Tank	20 gals
Cooling System	19½ qts
Tires	7.10 x 15
Suspension	front: ind, coil springs
	rear: solid axle, leaf springs
Frame	mono body
Transmission	3-speed manual (standard)
	overdrive (optional)
	Hydra-Matic (optional)
Rear Axle Ratio	3.58:1
Price	$3,050
Owner	Dick and Dee Hitt/NJ

Accessories

Backup Lights
Automatic Battery Filler
Cigarette Lighter
Clock (Manual Windup) Electric Clock (Optional)
Directional Signals
Emergency Trouble Light
Fire Extinguisher
Fog Lamps
Hydraulic Jack
Karvisor (Front Windshield Sunshade)
Tissue Dispenser
Mirror (Outside Driver's Side; Vanity Mirror on Passenger Visor)
Radio (with Rear Speaker)
Rear Window Wiper
Spotlight
Steering Wheel Kit (18″) (Extra-size Steering Wheel)
Trunk Light
Under-Hood Light
Window Ventshades
Windshield Washer
Hubcap Kit
Spare Tire Valve Extension
Power Windows (Hydraulic)
Fender Skirts

1953 *Cadillac 62*

Tailfins that were graceful, a disappearing gas cap beneath the rear taillight on the driver's side, and those majestic, massive, bulletlike bumpers; by the mid 50s these projectiles became known as "Dagmars," after a female TV personality named Dagmar who had an ample pair of "Dagmars" herself.

"You can say what you want about those bumpers, but you never saw a Caddy with any front or rear dings or dents when they made those bumpers," said a friend who owned on in 1953.

But the 1953 Caddy was more than just a pair of great bumpers and a disappearing gas cap. At a time when most lower-priced cars were just that and so-called Euro-

Specifications

Overall Length	220.5″
Width	80″
Height	61.1″
Weight	4,500 lbs
Wheelbase	126″
Engine	OHV V-8 331 cid/5.4 liter
Carburetor	4 bbls
Horsepower	210 @ 4,500 rpm
Bore & Stroke	3.81 x 3.625
Compression Ratio	8.25:1
Electrical	12 volt
Fuel Tank	20 gals
Cooling System	19 qts (less heater)
Tires	8.00 x 15
Suspension	front: ind, coil springs, knee action shocks rear: solid axle, semielliptic springs
Frame	X-type
Transmission	automatic (Hydra-Matic)
Rear Axle Ratio	3.36:1 (3.07 option)
Price	$4,200
Owner	Roger Rohde/NJ

Accessories

Power Steering
Power Brakes
Power Windows
Power Seat
Power Antenna
Radio (Signal Seeking with Wonder Bar; Remote Foot Control [Optional])
Dual Exhaust
Leather Interior
Autronic Eye (Changes High Beams to Low and Then Back Automatically)
Electrically Heated Front Seats (Standard on Eldorado)
Air-Conditioning
Fog Lights
Antilock Brakes (After Market Dealer Installation)
Wire Wheels

pean luxury cars still did not know what a heater was, the 1953 Caddy had automatic transmission, power windows, power steering, power brakes, automatic headlight dimmer, power seats, power antenna, electrically heated seats, a full-sized trunk with a full-sized spare tire, room for six people, an ohv 331 cid V-8 engine made of almost indestructible iron, and a look that said, "$4,200; how could they possibly give you so much car that also looks great."

The ride, that Cadillac ride. What is so terrible about not feeling the road—the bumps, the cracks, the holes, the crevices? Ever notice how people with many of these so-called performance sedans, driving machines, super-luxury, feel-the-road, it-takes-a-computer-scientist-to-maintain-it cars not only have a stiff upper lip but a stiff upper back? The owner of a 1953 Caddy has a huge grin and a warm hello.

1953 Ford F-100 Pickup

The little red truck that could...go anywhere and knock 'em dead. The F-100 is a short-bed half-ton pickup, or pick-me-upper, or social pickup that has more class than any late model what's-it-you-call-'em with a price tag that is pure crass.

    This truck has been a working truck most of its

Specifications

Overall Length	188"
Width	77"
Height	72"
Weight	4,800 lbs (GVW)
Wheelbase	110"
Engine	flat-head V-8/239 cid/3.9 liter
Carburetor	2 bbls
Horsepower	106 @ 3,500 rpm
Bore & Stroke	3.187 x 3.75
Compression Ratio	6.8:1
Electrical	6 volt
Fuel Tank	17 gals
Cooling System	24.5 qts
Tires	6.50 x 15
Suspension	solid axle, leaf springs front and rear
Frame	full frame, ladder type
Transmission	3-speed manual
	4-speed manual (optional)
Rear Axle Ratio	3.92:1
Price	$1,350 (purchased on November 2, 1953 from Ted Schultz Auto Sales, Pearl River, NY)
Owner	Bob Shaffer/NJ

Accessories

Automatic Transmission (Optional)
Heater/Defroster (Optional)
Radio (Optional)
Fuel, Oil, Amps, and Temperature Gauges
Electric Clock (Optional)

entire life, which has been spent in New York. So you know this is one tough truck, for if you can make it here. . . .

In the mid-1980s Bob Shaffer, the truck's second owner, did a restoration. All the work was done by Bob in his one-car (or truck) garage adjacent to his house. Bob took the truck down to bare metal, primed and painted it, and performed all the mechanical work himself—with much understanding from his wife and son.

Bob does not consider it a spectacular feat that he did all the work himself, even though he is not a mechanic or body person. He's just about as unspectacular as his little red truck!

1954 Pontiac Star Chief

Except for some minor trim molding changes on the hood and running the length of the car, the 1954 Pontiac looked very similar to the 1953. There was one *big* difference, however; the Star Chief was a new series. It represented the top end of the Pontiac line. The wheelbase was two inches longer than the standard Chieftain line and the rear of the car was extended eleven inches. Leather was a choice option, not an extra cost item.

The Chieftain offered a choice of either the straight 6 cyl or straight 8 cyl, while the Star Chief came

28

Specifications

Overall Length	213.7″ Chieftain/202.75″ wagon/ 205.3″
Width	76.6″
Height	63.25″
Weight	3,551 lbs
Wheelbase	124″ Chieftain/122″
Engine	straight 8-cyl/268 cid/4.4 liter Star Chief
	straight 6-cyl/239.2 cid/3.9 liter Chieftain
Carburetor	2 bbls
Horsepower	8-cyl { 127 @ 3,800 rpm/automatic / 122 @ 3,800 rpm/manual
	6-cyl { 118 @ 3,800/automatic / 115 @ 3,800/manual
Bore & Stroke	3.375 x 3.75/8-cyl
	3.562 x 4.00/6-cyl
Compression Ratio	7.7:1
Electrical	6 volt
Fuel Tank	20 gals
Cooling System	20½ qts
Tires	7.10 x 15
Suspension	front: ind, coils springs, king pins rear: solid axle, leaf springs
Frame	full frame
Transmission	3-speed synchromesh Hydra-Matic (optional)
Rear Axle Ratio	3.23:1 Hydra-Matic
	4.1:1 manual/6 cyl
	3.9:1 manual/8 cyl
Price	$2,550
Owner	Jeff Steiger/NJ

Accessories

Power Steering
Power Brakes
Power Windows
Air-Conditioning
Backup Lights
Directional Signals
Heater/Defroster
Leather Interior
Fender Skirts
Windshield Washer
Continental Kit
Remote Control Outside Mirror
Under-Hood Light
Windshield Sun Visor
Fog Lights
Illuminated Hood Ornament
Power Antenna
Spot Light

only with the straight 8. This would be the last year of the whisper quiet, silky smooth straight 8. In 1955 Pontiac would return to a V-8, an engine it had not used since 1933. This would also be the last year of a 6-volt electrical system. Pontiac and Chevrolet would join the rest of the GM lineup in 1955 with 12-volt electrical systems (Buick, Cadillac, and Oldsmobile went to 12-volt in 1953).

As portholes were to Buick, so the Indian chief, Pontiac, whose head graces this car's hood, was to Pontiac. At night that head is illuminated when the car's lights are on—your own private pathfinder to lead the way. It made the Pontiac distinctive, something which seems to have been lost in new cars. There were also the five silver streaks on the Pontiac deck lid, as in Pontiac Silver Streak.

The name Silver Streak came into being in the late 1930s because of the use of the silver streaks on the hood. In some ads Pontiac referred to their car as the Silver Streak, after the train of the period.

1954 *Packard Panther*

Specifications

Overall Length	216″
Width	78″
Height	55″
Weight	4,000 lbs
Wheelbase	122″
Engine	straight 8-cyl 359 cid/5.8 liter
Carburetor	4 bbls
Horsepower	212 @ 4,000 rpm
Bore & Stroke	3.562 x 4.50
Compression Ratio	8.7:1
Electrical	6 volt
Fuel Tank	20 gals
Cooling System	19.9 qts
Tires	8.20 x 15
Suspension	front: ind, coil springs rear: solid axle, leaf springs
Frame	X-type
Transmission	automatic (Packard Ultramatic)
Rear Axle Ratio	3.54:1
Price	Dream car made by Packard—priceless in 1954 and priceless today
Owner	Fred Kanter/NJ

Accessories

Power Steering
Power Brakes
Heater/Defroster
Outside Mirror (Driver and Passenger Side)
Radio (AM)
Fuel, Oil, Amps, Temperature, and Manifold Pressure Gauges
Tachometer
Electric Clock

In the 1950s many of the automobile companies had special show cars made for the Motoramas that came to many cities displaying the new models for each year. These Motoramas also featured what the car designers called their "dream cars," or cars of the future.

One such car was the Packard Panther (sometimes referred to as Packard Daytona), seen here. The car was hand-built and featured styling and engineering that someday all Packards would have. The Panther was fifty-five inches high, which was, with the exception of sports cars, from seven to nine inches lower than any other production car of the day.

On the measured mile at Daytona in 1954 the Panther was clocked at 131.1 mph—not bad for a 4,000-pound, precomputer-technology car. The Panther used a minimal amount of chrome and just let the lines speak for themselves. It had a single bench seat for you and someone special, and a real trunk.

The car does have a top. It stows away out of sight under a lid that lifts up behind the seat. Fewer than eight Panthers were made in 1954. For 1955 Packard replaced the Willys-like taillight with the cathedral-like lights of the Packard Caribbean.

In 1956 Packard merged with Studebaker. The 1957 Packard was more of a Packardbaker, and 1958 was the last year of the name Packard. In its final year Packard/Studebaker offered an option on their V-8—a supercharger!

Packard called it both the Panther, which is on the car, and the Panther Daytona, after it raced on the track at Daytona.

1954 *Willys Aero*

T his is not a scaled-down version of a Cadillac (note the Cadillac-like rear taillights) or some customized Ford Falcon. It is a Willys Aero, as in Willys-Overland of Toledo, Ohio. Willys also made the Jeepster and the Jeep. Before Chrysler bought Jeep from American Motors, Jeep was owned by Kaiser. Henry Kaiser bought Willys-Overland in 1954 and the following year, 1955, was the last for the Willys. The poor-selling Willys Aero, first introduced in 1952, was scratched by Kaiser who decided to keep the profitable Jeep.

Willys-Overland had a long history of being a kind of maverick in the auto world. Prior to World War II it made small American cars when no one else did. With World War II they made the Jeep, which is still being made today along the same lines. Some things are truly better off left as they are, and the Jeep is definitely one of these.

When World War II came to an end, Willys decided to stay with its Jeep and market it to civilians. Passenger car production was not resumed. In 1948 the Jeepster was introduced. This was a sporty two-wheel-drive version of a Jeep, which held four passengers.

The year 1952 saw Willys's reentry into the passenger car market with the Aero. It was only 183 inches long, weighed 2,778 lbs, and got about 25–30 mpg. It held six people very comfortably and their luggage too. In 1952 Willys sold a little over 31,000 cars. In 1953 it was 42,200. In 1954 this dropped to just under 12,000, and in 1955, the final year for the Aero (and the public knew it), only 6,654 were turned out by the factory. In its four-year run 92,046 Willys passenger cars were produced.

The Willys seen here is truly a remarkable car with an equally remarkable owner. Urban Haddocks bought the car new in 1954. "We [Urban and his wife] bought this car in Brooklyn on Broadway and Mrytle Avenues. It was a machine supply store with tractors and other machinery on display. There was only one Willys, this Aero model. We were going to drive to Florida and my wife didn't want to go in the Packard . . . the ride was too hard and the heater was not working that well any more (the Packard was a 1934, which was bought new) and the steering was hard. The Willys had power steering, it was smaller than the Packard, and I remember they made a damn good car in the 30s. We picked the Aero up a few days later and that weekend we drove to Florida. After staying in Florida a while, my wife wanted to see California so we drove there and then back to New York City. We drove every year to Florida with the car and then in 1984 my wife wanted to see the United States again, so we drove to all forty-eight states. I do not know how many people can brag about that and do it in a thirty-year-old car. It is such a sweet car,

Specifications

Overall Length	183"
Width	72"
Height	60½"
Weight	2,778 lbs (shipping weight) 2,925 lbs (curb weight) *
Wheelbase	108"
Engine	L-head 6-cyl 226 cid/3.7 liter
Carburetor	1 bbl
Horsepower	115 @ 3,600 rpm
Bore & Stroke	3.312 x 4.375
Compression Ratio	7.3:1
Electrical	6 volt
Fuel Tank	18 gals
Cooling System	11½ qts
Tires	6.40 x 15
Suspension	front: ind, coil springs rear: solid axle, semielliptic leaf springs
Frame	unit body
Transmission	automatic (standard with Ace Deluxe) 3-speed manual (standard on Lark and Ace) overdrive (optional) Hydra-Matic (optional)
Rear Axle Ratio	3.31:1
Price	$2,023
Owner	Urban Haddocks/NY

Accessories

Power Steering
Heater/Defroster
Air Cleaner (with Oil Bath)
Brass Radiator
Electric Clock
Radio

*See Glossary, page 143

never gave me an ounce of trouble in all these years. You know it is all original. Aside from changing the tires and battery, the paint, interior, chrome, everything on the car is original. Just change the oil every 1,500 to 2,000 miles, put a new battery in every five years, and tune-ups every 6,000 miles or so, and she just keeps humming along. Two years ago my wife died . . . you live long enough that is what happens. Now I go to a couple of [car] shows a year with the car. To some people it may be just a car or a piece of machinery, but you know she really has a personality all her own. My wife liked this car . . . she has been good to us over the years; isn't that all you can ask of anybody?"

The Willys line of passenger cars consisted of the Aero Lark, Aero Ace, and Ace Deluxe, the top-of-the-line four-door sedan. In two-door hardtop form the Ace Deluxe was called the Eagle, and in 1955 it would be known as the Bermuda. Except for side trim moldings the 1954 and 1955 models are almost identical. In the first year of production the front windshield was two-piece; in 1953 it became a one-piece unit. In 1954 there were a few cars that came from Willys with the Paxton centrifugal supercharger, which produced 140 hp.

Willys also came up with the idea of having the windshield wipers moving in the same direction, elmininating the blind spot in the center. This was somehow accomplished despite the fact that there was no computer available at the time.

The front coil springs were set up in a way similar to the Rambler (though unconventional by most standards): The coils were placed above the upper suspension control arm rather than between the upper and lower arms. This reduced unsprung weight and provided for better lateral stability. Willys was also one of the first car makers to use front wheels with a wider tread than the rear, which results in greater stability.

1955 *Imperial*

For 1955 the elegant Imperial was finally allowed to stand on its own, apart from Chrysler. It was no longer a Chrysler Imperial, but Imperial. From its richly detailed front grille to its distinctive free-standing gun-sight taillights, the Imperial has "elegance" stamped all over it.

Rich broadcloths and fine leather accentuate the interior of this living room on wheels. In fact, the Imperial was probably a good deal more comfortable than many homes of that era—it had air-conditioning! From any angle the Imperial stands out with its clean, elegant lines,

Specifications

Overall Length	223"
Width	79.1"
Height	61.5"
Weight	4,490 lbs
Wheelbase	130"
Engine	OHV hemi V-8 331 cid/5.4 liter
Carburetor	4 bbls
Horsepower	250 @ 4,600 rpm
Bore & Stroke	3.81 x 3.63
Compression Ratio	8.5:1
Electrical	6 volt
Fuel Tank	20 gals
Cooling System	25 qts
Tires	8.20 x 15
Suspension	front: ind, coil springs
	rear: solid axle, leaf springs
Frame	side rail
Transmission	automatic (Powerflite)
Rear Axle Ratio	3.31:1
Price	$4,700
Owner	Salvatore Anicito/NJ

(0–60 mph in 11 seconds)

Accessories

Power Steering
Power Brakes
Power Windows
Power Seat
Outside Mirror (Driver's and Passenger Side)
Air-Conditioning
Radio *Town & Country*
Power Antenna
Trip Odometer
Fuel, Oil, Amps and Temperature Gauges)
Electric Clock
Wire Wheels
Tinted Glass
Heater/Defroster
Two-Tone Paint
Fog Lights
Spotlight
Windshield Washer
Dual Exhaust

not even disrupted by an unsightly gas filler door. Like the Cadillac, the Imperial had its gas filler hidden . . . beneath the taillight on the passenger side.

In limousine form the Imperial is known as the Crown Imperial, with a wheelbase of 149½ inches and an overall length of 249 inches. The Crown series also had disc brakes. This would be the last year for disc brakes, until they would appear again in 1967 on all Imperial models.

Besides the Crown series, the Imperial was only offered in a four-door sedan and a two-door hardtop. In 1956 a four-door hardtop would be added, and in 1957 Imperial was finally given a convertible.

With its 331 cid Hemi V-8, extended hours of high-speed cruising was a simple task for the Imperial. Although it was a big land yacht of a car, the Imperial still managed to get 15–17 mpg.

Here was a car for the connoisseur, the person of means who wanted a distinctively elegant automobile.

1955 *Studebaker President Speedster*

enry and Clement Studebaker started out making Conestoga wagons in South Bend, Indiana. Studebakers were produced here until 1965, when operations were moved to Canada. In 1966 the Canadian plant was shut down as well. In 1953, Studebaker's one hundredth year in the vehicle business, Studebaker came out with their low-slung, European-inspired, Raymond Loewy-designed Starliner. In 1955 Studebaker decided to revive the President name (which had been dropped in the late 1930s) in the form of a luxurious four-door sedan and a beautifully outrageous sport coupe. Retaining the silhouette of the Starliner, the car was enhanced (or destroyed, depending upon whose eye is beholding the beauty) by a

Specifications

Overall Length	204½"
Width	70½"
Height	57½"
Weight	3,300 lbs
Wheelbase	120½"
Engine	OHV V-8 259 cid/4.2 liter
Carburetor	4 bbls
Horsepower	185 @ 4,500 rpm
Bore & Stroke	3.562 x 3.25
Compression Ratio	7.5:1
Electrical	6 volt
Fuel Tank	18 gals
Cooling System	18.75 qts
Tires	7.10 x 15
Suspension	front: ind, coil springs
	rear: solid axle, leaf springs
Frame	steel box section
Transmission	automatic
Rear Axle Ratio	3.554:1
Price	$3,253
Owner	Bob Ruby/NJ

(2,215 President Speedster hardtops were built. This car is body #67, built in January 1955.)

Accessories

Power Steering
Power Brakes
Automatic Transmission
Heater/Defroster
Power Seat
Radio (AM Only Type Available)
Fuel, Oil, Amps, and Temperature Gauges
Tachometer
Electric Clock
Power Windows
Fog Lights
Under-Hood Lights
Windshield Washer
Color: Sun Valley Yellow/Hialeah Green

massive chrome grill and bumper, chrome bar over the roof, and unique two- or three-tone paint combinations.

The interior of the car was definitely upscale, from the special tufted leather to the engine-turned dash, which is reminiscent of the coach-built cars of the 1930s. The Speedster hardtop was a personal-type car long before the word came into use for cars that have very little style but a major price. Very few persons can afford them or really want them.

On cars equipped with the manual transmission, Studebaker offered a unique option—the Hill Holder. This device provided braking power on a hill without keeping a foot on the brake pedal. When it was time to shift into gear, one foot went to the clutch and the other to the gas pedal without worry of the car rolling downhill backward.

A car with flair, the 1955 Studebaker President Speedster is racy looking—full of zest and vigor, like a flight into the future.

1955 Nash Rambler

Originally introduced in 1951, the Nash Rambler
Country Club received a face lift in 1955. Gone
were covered wheel wells in the front, which now
allowed for a wider front tread. The result was even better
handling for a car that was already superb. The car was
also more "squarish" (as some of the owners were made

Specifications

Overall Length	178½"/2-door 186¼"/4-door and wagon (continental kit add 7")
Width	73"
Height	59⅜"/2-door and 4-door 60½"/wagon
Weight	2,700 lbs
Wheelbase	100" (2-door) 108" (4-door and wagon)
Engine	L-head 6-cyl 195.6 cid/3.2 liter
Carburetor	1 bbl
Horsepower	90 @ 3,800 rpm
Bore & Stroke	3.125 x 4.25
Compression Ratio	7.3:1
Electrical	6 volt
Fuel Tank	20 gals
Cooling System	12 qts
Tires	6.40 x 15
Suspension:	front: ind, coil springs rear: solid axle, coil springs
Frame	unit body
Transmission	3-speed manual overdrive (optional) Hydra-Matic (optional)
Rear Axle Ratio	3.77:1 manual 4.40:1 overdrive 3.30:1 Hydra-Matic
Price	$1,700
Owner	Leonard Shiller/NY

Accessories

Power Steering (Optional)
Power Brakes (Optional)
Heater/Defroster (Optional)
Air-Conditioning (Optional)
Outside Mirror Driver's Side (Standard)
Radio (AM Optional)
Fuel, Oil, Amps, and Temperature Gauges (Standard)
Electric Clock (Optional)
Continental Kit (Standard)
Reclining Front Seat (Standard)

out to be: the complete nerd's car). Gone was the bathtub look.

Ramblers were more than just small, economical automobiles; they were small luxury cars. From their reclining front seats to air-conditioning, here was a car that delivered 25 mpg, seated six people very comfortably, was capable of cruising at 75 mph all day, was simple to service and fun to drive, all at a very reasonable price.

Just take a good look at this car—the color, the style, that Continental kit on the rear. This car is more than cute; it's gorgeous! The car is a true performance machine. That 195 cid 6-cyl engine is indestructible. The car always starts no matter what the weather conditions, and it never fails to keep running. There was a song written about Ramblers in the mid-50s named "Beep, Beep," by the Playmates. If you can listen to it somewhere, someday, do so.

This particular Rambler has been in New York City its entire life, which means in car years it is one hundred years old. As for "the complete nerd's car," some of the so-called nerds had the last laugh with the Rambler's reclining, make-into-a-bed front seats. Nash even offered screens as an option to keep out insects when parked on warm nights.

In addition to several late '50s Cadillacs, I also own a 1963 Rambler Classic 770 station wagon with the 195 cid 6-cyl.

1955 Cadillac Eldorado

The Eldorado, which made its debut in 1952, was an ultra luxurious Cadillac offered only as a convertible. That first year the Eldorado was available only in white lacquer with contrasting red and white leather interior. The 1953 model looked just like the 1952, except it now had a dip in the door and came with wire wheels

Specifications

Overall Length	223.3"
Width	80"
Height	60"
Weight	4,800 lbs
Wheelbase	129"
Engine	OHV V-8 331 cid/5.4 liter
Carburetor	dual quads/2–4 bbls
Horsepower	270 @ 4,800 rpm
Bore & Stroke	3.812 x 3.625
Compression Ratio	9.0:1
Electrical	12 volt
Fuel Tank	20 gals
Cooling System	20.75 qts
Tires	8.00 x 15
Suspension	front: ind, coil springs, king pins rear: solid axle, leaf springs
Frame	X-member with "A" box
Transmission	automatic (Hydra-Matic)
Rear Axle Ratio	3.36:1 3.07:1 (optional)
Price	$6,300
Owner	Michael Bronson/NY

Accessories

Power Steering
Power Brakes
Power Windows
Power Seat
Leather Interior
Heater/Defroster
Air-Conditioning
Radio (with Rear Speaker)
Power Antenna
Remote Trunk Release
Remote-Controlled Mirror (Driver's Side)
Trip Odometer
Tinted Glass
Electric Clock
Windshield Washer
Gold Grille (Optional)
5 Saber Spoke Wheels (Standard) (Gold Optional)
Fog Lamps
Whitewall Tires
Metal Tonneau Cover
Autronic Eye (Headlight Dimmer)

instead of wheel covers. The Eldorado was also distinctively different than the standard Cadillac with its unique curved windshield. For model year 1954, it appears Cadillac did not know where it was heading with the Eldorado and the car was differentiated from the standard series 62 convertible primarily by stainless steel skirts and trim along the lower rear quarter panel.

In 1955 Eldorado definitely seemed to know where it was going. From its unique rear end treatment, which was three years ahead in style from the rest of the Cadillac line, to its dual quad carburetors under the hood and sabre spoke wheels, the Eldorado stood apart from the Cadillac line—as well as from the rest of the car world. Also absent from the 1955 Eldorado were skirts. For the first time since the 1930s there was a Cadillac without skirts. In 1959 the Eldorado would again be properly dressed with its own set of skirts.

The 1956 Eldorado would differ only in the treatment of its front grill and Dagmars (they would be about an inch and a half shorter, from about a 38D to a 36D). The dual exhausts that were mounted in the rear bumper would be vertical in 1956 as opposed to circular in 1955. On the standard Cadillac the exhaust opening would be horizontal in 1956. In addition to the convertible there would now be a two-door hardtop Eldorado named the Seville (see pages 66–67).

(The only options on the Eldorado were the gold grille, gold saber spoke wheels, and air-conditioning. And you had to choose a color.)

1956 Cadillac Coupe de Ville

I f there are two words that best sum up the overall spirit and emotion of the 50s they are "pink Cadillac." Elvis Presley had several pink Cadillacs; Jayne Mansfield, a "blond bombshell" from the 50s, had one; and Roy Kahn owns the one you see here.

    "I was in St. Louis on business in the summer of 1988 riding on a two-lane, two-way country road," he says. "Approaching me—I could not believe my eyes—was this

Specifications

Overall Length	221.9" (series 62 sedan/214.9")
	(Fleetwood/225.9")
Width	80"
Height	59.6"
Weight	4,850 lbs
Wheelbase	129" (Fleetwood/133")
Engine	OHV V-8 365 cid/6.0 liter
Carburetor	4 bbls
Horsepower	285 @ 4,600 rpm
	305 @ 4,700 rpm (Eldorado)
Bore & Stroke	4" x 3.625"
Compression Ratio	9.75:1
Electrical	12 volt
Fuel Tank	20 gals
Cooling System	19.5 qts
Tires	8.00 x 15
Suspension	front: ind, coil springs, king pins
	rear: solid axle leaf springs, forked
	arms
Frame	X-member with "A" box
Transmission	Hydra-Matic (4-speed automatic)
Rear Axle Ratio	3.07:1
Price	$4,569 (base price + options)
Owner	Roy Kahn/NY

1956 pink and grey Cadillac Coupe de Ville.* My uncle had one when I was eight. I never forgot that car; my mother loved it too. My father was more practical and thought the car too big and flashy. Anyway, I jammed on my brakes, made a U-turn, and followed this car. The elderly gentleman driving it finally pulled into a small mini mall and I got my chance to get out and talk to him. He said he was not ready to sell the car yet, but he would take my phone number and keep me in mind. For the next several months I discovered I had to be in St. Louis more frequently. The moment I saw that car I knew I had to have it, I wanted it . . . I was ready to move to St. Louis.

"In the spring of 1989, the gentleman who owned the car told me on my most recent trip to St. Louis that his eyes were starting to go a little. He could tell how much I liked the car, and well, if I wanted—if I wanted, he asked! —he would sell me the car. I was both happy and sad at once. I was finally getting my dream car, but this man had bought the car new, and it was more than a machine to him, and I was grateful for the fact he appreciated how much I loved the car too.

"I came back in two weeks with my wife and we drove back to New York."

From its massive bumpers to its concealed gas filler in the taillight on the driver's side and air-conditioning intakes mounted on the top of the rear fenders, the 1956 Cadillac—especially in pink—was some sight to behold when new and is even more so today.

The car could go from 0–60 in eleven seconds, cruise at 80 mph all day, and had a top speed of 122 mph. Sitting in this car was like being in a living room on wheels, and with air-conditioning it was just as comfortable no

*Mountain Laurel Pink/Camelot Grey—author

Accessories

Power Steering (Standard)
Power Brakes (Standard)
Power Windows (Standard)
Power Seat (Standard)
Heater/Defroster (Standard)
Radio with Rear Speaker (Standard)
Power Antenna (Standard)
Remote Trunk Release (Optional)
Air-Conditioning (Optional)
Outside Mirror Driver's Side—Remote-Controlled (Standard)
Trip Odometer
Automatic Headlight Dimmer (Optional)
Tinted Glass (Standard)
Tinted Windshield (Standard)
Electric Clock (Standard)
Windshield Washer (Standard)
Fuel and Temperature Gauges
Gold Grill (Optional)
5 Gold Sabre Spoke Wheels (Optional)
Fog Lamps (Optional)
Passenger Side Sun Visor Vanity Mirror with Cadillac Logo (Optional)
Leather Interior (Optional)
Dual Exhaust (Standard)

matter what the weather. For the first time, air-conditioning was available on the Cadillac convertible too.

The 1956 Cadillac was similar to the 1955 and 1954 models, except for some minor trim and the protrusion of the side moldings along the rear quarter panels. All decked out as the 1956 is here with its options, the Coupe de Ville went for $5,800.

As the song written by Bruce Springsteen goes:

We don't have to go anywhere
We'll just park it in the back
And have a party in your pink Cadillac

1956 *Plymouth Belvedere*

T urqoise and white two-tone paint, fender skirts, wire wheel covers, of course some dice over the rearview mirror, and this car has "take me to the beach" written all over it. This was the second year of Chrysler Corporation's "Forward Look." (In 1957 an advertising line would be added: "Suddenly it's 1960.")

During this period, the golden (or chrome) age of American cars, the automakers were always promising the future and good times in their ads. One of the futuristic

Specifications

Overall Length	204.8"
Width	74.6"
Height	60.1"
Weight	3,450 lbs
Wheelbase	115"
Engine	OHV V-8 277 cid/4.5 liter
	L-head 6-cyl 230 cid/3.7 liter
	OHV V-8 268 cid/4.4 liter
	OHV V-8 303 cid/5 liter (Fury engine)
Carburetor/ Horsepower	4 bbls (277 V-8) 187 bhp @ 4,400 rpm
	1 lbbl (6-cyl) 125 bhp @ 3,600 rpm
	2 bbls (268 V-8) 180 bhp @ 4,400 rpm
	2–4 bbls (303 V-8) 260 bhp @ 4,800 rpm
Bore & Stroke	3.75" x 3.13" (277 V-8)
	3.63" x 3.25" (268 V-8)
	3.25" x 4.63" (6-cyl)
	3.81" x 3.31" (303 V-8)
Compression Ratio	8.0:1
	8.0:1
	7.6:1
	9.25:1
Electrical	12 volt
Fuel Tank	17 gals
Cooling System	20 qts/V-8
	14 qts/6-cyl
Tires	6.70 x 15
Suspension	front: ind, coil springs
	rear: solid axle, semielliptic leaf springs
Frame	full box with two cross members
Transmission	3-speed manual
	overdrive (optional)
	Power Flite (optional)
Rear Axle Ratio	3.75:1/manual
	4.10:1/overdrive
	3.54:1/Power Flite
Price	$2,500
Owner	Vic Coiro/NY

items on the 1956 Plymouth was the Highway Hi-Fi. This was a specially constructed shock-resistant record player that played a special seven-inch-size record.

This was a CRUISIN' car—a car that made going for a container of ice cream a vacation. Going anywhere in this car was fun. If you wanted performance it was there, no doubt about it, in the form of dual quads—two four-barrel carburetors as a factory option for the OHV 303 cid V-8. That is, if the basic 277 cid V-8 was not enough.

Ever notice how many car ads today talk about and show cars from the past, and usually that past is a '50s dream machine? Take a good look at this Plymouth Belvedere. This car is the future.

Accessories

Power Steering
Power Brakes
Heater/Defroster
Window Washer
Outside Mirror (Driver and Passenger side)
Tachometer
Fuel, Oil, Amps, and Temperature Gauges
Radio
Highway Hi-Fi
Rear Fender Skirts
Wire Wheel Covers
Seat Belts (Front and Rear)
Directional Signals
Backup Lights
Air-Conditioning
Two-Tone Paint

1956 *Lincoln Premiere*

The hot Lincolns of Mexican road race fame (1952 to 1954) were well known for their performance and durability but lacked a little in the luxury touch both in design and interior appointments.

All this changed in 1956. The 1956 Lincoln was seven inches longer than the 1955 and four inches lower. It was/is beautiful. To confirm this the Industrial Designers Institute awarded Lincoln for its "excellence in automotive design" in 1956.

The '56 Lincoln not only looked good but performed well and was safe. The car had a new collapsing

Specifications

Overall Length	222.9"
Width	79.9"
Height	58" (sedan/60")
Weight	4,452 lbs
Wheelbase	126"
Engine	OHV V-8 368 cid/6-liter
Carburetor	4 bbls
Horsepower	285 @ 4,600 rpm
Bore & Stroke	4.00" x 3.66"
Compression Ratio	9.00:1
Electrical	12 volt
Fuel Tank	20 gals
Cooling System	25.2 qts
Tires	8.20 x 15
Suspension	front: ind, coil springs, ball joints rear: solid axle, semielliptic leaf springs
Frame	X-type
Transmission	automatic (Turbo Drive)
Rear Axle Ratio	3.07:1
Price	$4,767
Owner	Jim Ragsdale/NJ

(Production: 2,400 convertibles)

Accessories

Power Steering
Power Brakes
Power Windows
Power Vent Windows
Power Seat
Radio with Rear Speaker
Power Antenna
Air-Conditioning
Heater/Defroster (with Separate Controls for Front and Rear)
Leather Interior
Seat Belts (Front and Rear)
Fog Lamps
Remote Trunk Release
Power Door Locks
Auto Lube—Built-In Self-Lubricating System
Automatic Headlight Dimmer
Continental Kit
Electric Clock
Fuel, Oil, Amp, and Temperature Gauges
Color: Island Coral

safety steering wheel. Upon sudden impact the wheel collapses and absorbs the impact of the driver. The Lincoln also had both front and rear seat belts.

The engine had more power due to an increase to 368 cid from 341 cid in 1955. The interiors were more plush, with extensive use of leather and fine fabrics.

Then there were the color offerings: soft pastels in pinks, green, turquoise, blue, and island coral—the color seen here. Try to picture this color on any car made today. Doesn't work, does it? There is more to paint than just the color; there has to be a design underneath it.

49

1957 *Chrysler* 300C

Muscle car! In 1955 Chrysler introduced a new series called the 300. It had 300 horsepower. In 1956 it was called the 300B. (There was no letter designation in 1955.) The first 300 had a 331 cid with dual quads; in 1956 displacement was increased to 354 with dual quads; and in 1957 that engine grew to the 392 cid hemi with dual quads. With the optional 10.0:1 compression ratio, stick shift, and no power options this setup put

50

Specifications

Overall Length	219.2″
Width	78.8″
Height	54.7″ (convertible 55″)
Weight	4,235 lbs
Wheelbase	126″
Engine	OHV V-8 hemi 392 cid/5.9 liter
Carburetor	2–4 bbls
Horsepower	375 @ 5,200 rpm
Bore & Stroke	4″ x 3.90″
Compression Ratio	9.25:1
Electrical	12 volt
Fuel Tank	23 gals
Cooling System	25 qts
Tires	9.00 x 14
Suspension	front: ind, torsion bar
	rear: 7 longitudinal leaf springs
Frame	full frame
Transmission	Automatic (Torque Flite)
Rear Axle Ratio	3.31:1
Price	$4,929
Owner	Richard Dangler/NY

(top speed: 135+ mph)

Accessories

Power Steering
Power Brakes
Heater/Defroster
Electrical Clock
Power Seat
Outside Mirror (Driver's Side)
Power Windows
Air-Conditioning
Radio
Power Antenna
Rear Window Defogger (Blower Type)
Fuel, Oil, Amps, and Temperature Gauges
Highway Hi-Fi
Trip Odometer
Seat Belts

out 390 hp at 5,400 rpm. With the standard compression of 9.25:1 and 375 hp, the car was capable of a measured mile speed of 145.7 mph. This in a car that weighed a little over two tons, held four people very comfortably in their individual leather bucket seats, and had a trunk that could hold a Yugo.

The Chrysler 300C is also one of the best proportioned big cars ever made in a design of understated elegance. From front to back and side to side, there is not one angle from which the car does not look great. The 300C went from 0–60 mph in 7.7 seconds and at 100 mph had plenty of acceleration left.

The car is a marvel of engineering, not only from a power point of view, but in everyday driving. Unless that second carb is opened up when the pedal hits the metal, the car just acts smoothly and demurely.

It was rumored that the front grille design was not for taking in fresh air as most people thought, but for eating anything that got in the 300's way, and then it would spew the remains out its dual exhaust.

1957 *Mercury Turnpike Cruiser*

The audacity of a car to bill itself as the Turnpike Cruiser! But with its 368 cid and 4 bbls carb, this car was a real cruiser! Add to that the optional 2–4 bbls on this engine, and there was not enough turnpike left to tame this "Big M." In 1957 a Mercury Turnpike Cruiser convertible was the Indianapolis 500 Pace Car in Sunglitter Yellow.

You step down into the new Mercury for 1957 due to the use of the new longitudinal side sections that are kicked out fourteen inches over the 1956 frame. This results in an overall height reduction of three inches. Yet the car has the same amount of headroom as the previous year's design.

The Cruiser was distinguishable from the standard Mercury by its quad headlights, fresh air intakes above the windshield, and, in hardtop form, the electrically operated rear window that was retractable all the way down. The control for this window was by the driver, so there was no fear of children playing with the window.

Among the many options that were available on the Cruiser were air suspension and memory seat. In addition to the many different positions the seat had, it also had a "memory" for two preset positions. If someone other than the owner had driven the car, all he or she had to do was push either of the two memory buttons for their favorite position and the seat would automatically return to that setting.

Like some other cars of this time, the Mercury had push-button transmission mounted on the left of the

Specifications

Overall Length	211.1"
Width	79.1"
Height	56.4"
Weight	4,222 lbs
Wheelbase	122"
Engine	OHV V-8 368 cid/6.0 liter
	OHV V-8 312 cid/5.1 liter
	(Monterey & Montclair)
Carburetor	4 bbls
Horsepower	290 @ 4,600 rpm 368 V-8
	255 @ 4,600 rpm 312 V-8
Bore & Stroke	4.00" x 3.65" 368 V-8
	3.80" x 3.44" 312 V-8
Compression Ratio	9.70:1 368 V-8
	9.70:1 312 V-8
Electrical	12 volt
Fuel Tank	20 gals
Cooling System	25.5 qts
Tires	8.00 x 14
Suspension	front: ind, unequal A-arms, coil springs, ball joints
	rear: solid axle, longitudinal leaf springs
Frame	ladder type with box-section side rails
Transmission	3-speed automatic torque converter with planetary gears (Merc-O-Matic)
	3-speed manual (standard on Monterey)
	overdrive (optional)
Rear Axle Ratio	3.22:1
Price	$3,900
Owner	Tom Jabaut/NJ

(Luggage Capacity/Trunk 31 cu. ft.)

Accessories

Power Steering
Power Brakes
Power Windows
Air-Conditioning
Automatic Transmission
Radio with Rear Speaker
Sliding Door Locks
Retractable Rear Window Electrically Controlled by Driver
Power Antenna
Power Seat with Memory
Tachometer
Compass
Electric Clock
Dual Exhaust
Quad Headlights
Continental Kit
Fuel, Oil, Amps, and Temperature Gauges
Trip Odometer
Cruiser Fender Skirts
Seat Belts

Color: Sunglitter, Special Turnpike Cruiser Paint, Pale Yellow

dash. There was a special lockout that prevented the accidental engagement of reverse above 10 mph. The buttons were mechanical, not electrically operated as on some other makes.

If it were judged on driver visibility alone, the Mercury would qualify as one of the safest cars made. With its hardtop styling and thin roof pillars, there are no blind spots. The driver does not have to lean back and forth, roll his head or make any other contortionlike moves to see forward, sideways, or to the rear.

Put this all together in a package with cruiser skirts, two-tone paint, and wide whites, and if every night were Saturday night there still would not be enough Saturday's in a week for this car and its owner.

54

1957 *Imperial*

In the early days of the auto industry the word "Imperial" meant a large, formal, closed car. This was at a time when almost all cars were open cars—not convertibles, but open, as in no top. If there was a top at all, it was just a wooden frame with some canvas or other material draped across it. There were no windows on the sides; these cars were open.

During the 1920s Chrysler began to designate its largest 6-cylinder series by the name of Imperial (the 1929 Chrysler Imperial was $2,975). As pointed out earlier in this book, it was not until 1955 that Chrysler Corporation finally allowed the Imperial to stand on its own and be an entirely separate division and car from Chrysler.

For 1957 Imperial was a completely redesigned car from the previous year, as were all the Chrysler Corporation automobiles. "Suddenly it is 1960" was the theme behind the entire Chrysler lineup, and the Imperial was the epitome of this look. The Imperial is free of meaningless bulges, ridges, dips, and chrome. For a car of this era the Imperial exercised restraint in its use of chrome. The tail-

Specifications

Overall Length	224″
Width	81″
Height	57½″
Weight	4,759 lbs
Wheelbase	129″
Engine	OHV V-8 hemi 392 cid/6.4 liter
Carburetor	4 bbls
Horsepower	325 @ 4,600 rpm
Bore & Stroke	4.0″ x 3.9″
Compression Ratio	9.25:1
Electrical	12 volt
Fuel Tank	23 gals
Cooling System	25 qts
Tires	9.50 x 14
Suspension	front: ind, torsion bar
	rear: solid axle, leaf springs
Frame	full frame, box section
Transmission	automatic (Torque-Flite/push-button)
Rear Axle Ratio	3.18:1
Price	$4,850
Owner	Robert Nixon/NJ
Color	Parade Green/Cloud White

Accessories

Power Steering (Standard)
Power Brakes (Standard)
Power Windows
Air-Conditioning
Heater/Defroster
Electric Clock
Power Seat
Outside Mirror Driver's Side (Remote-Controlled)
Outside Mirror Passenger Side (Remote-Controlled)
Transistorized Radio with Rear Speaker
Power Antenna
Rear Window Defogger
Power Door Locks
Trip Odometer
Fuel, Oil, Amps, and Temperature Gauges
Highway Hi-Fi Record Player
Seat Belts

fins seem part of the overall design of the car and not just added on.

The Imperial lineup for 1957 included a two-door hardtop, four-door hardtop, four-door sedan, the Crown limousine, and, for the first time since the 1930s, an Imperial convertible. Among the '57's features was a transistorized radio, which meant instant music the second the radio was turned on as opposed to the minute or so of warm-up time with a tube radio. There was also the Highway Hi-Fi record player, the push-button Torque-Flite transmission, and a front torsion bar for a soft, smooth ride.

The spare tire on the trunk lid was an option. It gave the car a touch of elegance and continental styling. Unfortunately, that is all it did: The tire was mounted inside the trunk.

As for performance, the Imperial could go from 0–60 mph in 10 seconds, with a top speed of 120 mph, while getting 11 mpg in city traffic and 17 mpg on the highway, which is better than the "big" Mercedes that is advertised today.

The Imperial you see here is truly a personal car. It has only what the original owner wanted. This car is equipped with power steering, power brakes, automatic transmission, and air-conditioning. It does not have a power seat or power windows. Dual headlights were optional. In 1958 virtually all American cars would have dual headlights as standard equipment.

There were no "packages" as there are today when you ordered your 1957 Imperial. You did not have to get $2,000 of worthless options when you only wanted one or two items.

As an ad for the 1957 Imperial goes, it was "a lesson in elegance."

1957 *Ford Skyliner*

A car with a steel roof which, at the press of a button, starts to lift itself up, makes a fold in the front and a bend in the back, while at the same time the trunk lid lifts itself upward and backward until the steel top lowers itself into the trunk, which has a special storage area for the top, which is then covered by the trunk lid. Sound very futuristic or like some type of fantasy?

It is neither from the future nor a fantasy; it is from the past. From 1957 to 1959 is when the Skyliner series was made by Ford. With the top down there was one

Specifications

Overall Length	210.7" Skyliner
	201.6" Custom series
	207.8" Fairlane series
	203.5" station wagons
Width	77"
Height	56.2" Skyliner/Fairlane
	57.1" Custom series
Weight	4,000 lbs
Engine	OHV V-8 312 cid/5.1 liter (Skyliner)
	OHV V-8 292 cid/4.8 liter (Fairlane)
	OHV V-8 272 cid/4.5 liter (Custom)
	OHV 6-cyl 223 cid/3.6 liter (Custom)
Carburetor	1 bbl 6-cyl
	4 bbls all V-8's
	2–4 bbls (option on 312 V-8)
Horsepower	144 @ 4,200 rpm 6-cyl
	190 @ 4,500 rpm 272 V-8
	212 @ 4,500 rpm 292 V-8
	245 @ 4,500 rpm 312 V-8
Bore & Stroke	3.62" x 3.60" 6-cyl
	3.62" x 3.30" 272 V-8
	3.75" x 3.30" 292 V-8
	3.80" x 3.44" 312 V-8
Compression Ratio	8.6:1 6-cyl/272 V-8
	9.0:1 292 V-8
	9.7:1 312 V-8
Electrical	12 volt
Fuel Tank	19 gals
Cooling System	20 qts
Tires	8.00 x 14
Suspension	front: ind, coil springs
	rear: solid axle, leaf springs
Frame	full frame, longitudinal side rails
Transmission	3-speed manual (standard)
	overdrive (optional)
Rear Axle Ratio	3.10:1 Ford-O-Matic
	3.65:1 manual
	3.70:1 overdrive
Price	$2,942
Owner	Al Burrows/NJ
Color	Starmist Blue/Colonial White

Accessories

Power Steering
Power Brakes
Power Windows
Heater/Defroster
Automatic Transmission
Air-Conditioning
Electric Clock
AM Radio with Rear Speaker
Power Antenna
Rear Window Defogger (Blower Type)
Continental Tire
Fender Skirts
Power Seat
Outside Mirror (Driver's Side and Passenger Side)
Two-Tone Paint
Seat Belts (Front and Rear Seats)

long, clean sweep of car from front to back, no telltale boot or convertible top protruding from behind the rear seat.

The first year the Skyliner sold 20,766 units. The same year, the soft-top convertible, the Sunliner, sold 77,000 cars, while the Thunderbird sold 21,000. Ford did not promote the Skyliner too much and in its three-year span sold 48,394 cars. Evidently Ford did not think the Skyliner's numbers indicated success or popularity. After 1959 there would be no more Skyliner—or any car like it. But the mechanism that powered the steel top was utilized in the Thunderbird convertible (which was a conventional soft-top) from 1958 through 1966, the last year of the Thunderbird convertible. The same principle and mechanics were applied to the four-door Lincoln Continental convertibles of 1961 to 1967.

The car is great and unique and when at half mast, together with its forward opening hood raised, it is definitely weird! Add a continental kit, a soft pastel blue known as Starmist blue with Colonial white, and a warm summer evening, and you truly have Super Joy!

1957 *Oldsmobile* 98

If you could not afford that pink Cadillac, an Olds 98 in pink was not a bad consolation prize. When you added the J-2/tri-power option to that 371 cid V-8, things really started looking good.

The J-2 was a unique multicarb arrangement. Under most normal conditions the middle carburetor was the only one functioning. Only under hard acceleration did the other two carburetors open up. When the throttle was opened three-fourths of the way, vacuum pressure would simultaneously open the outboard carburetors, feeding additional gas for a boost of power.

Specifications

Overall Length	216.7" (208.2"/88 series)
Width	76.4"
Height	58"
Weight	4,750 lbs
Wheelbase	126" (122"/88 series)
Engine	OHV V-8 371 cid/6.0 liter
Carburetor	4 bbls
	3–2 bbls (known as J-2 option)
Horsepower	277 @ 4,400 rpm 4 bbls
	300 @ 4,600 rpm J-2
Bore & Stroke	4" x 3.69"
Compression Ratio	9.5:1 4 bbls
	10.0:1 J-2
Electrical	12 volt
Fuel Tank	20 gals
Cooling System	21 qts
Tires	8.50 x 14
Suspension	front: ind., coil springs
	rear: solid axle, leaf springs
	outside of frame
Frame	X-type
Transmission	Hydra-Matic
Rear Axle Ratio	3.21:1
	3.42:1 (J-2)
Price	$3,900
Owner	Ken Flore/NY

Accessories

Power Steering
Power Brakes
Heater/Defroster
Blower-Type Rear Window Defogger (Not available on Convertible)
Power Seat
Remote-Controlled Mirror (Driver's Side)
Power Windows
Cruise Control (Buzzer Type)
AM Radio
Power Antenna
Trip Odometer
Fuel, Oil, Amps., and Temperature Gauges
Autronic Eye (Headlight Dimmer)
Electric Clock
Tinted Glass
Foot Control Radio Button
Air-Conditioning
Leather Interior
Dual Exhaust

Elliot "Pete" Estes, who was an engine development engineer at Oldsmobile, was transferred to Pontiac in October 1956. That was how Pontiac was introduced to its own tri-power setup.

Among the many options on the 1957 Olds was the "sportable" transistorized radio. This radio fit in the dash, just as any other radio, except you could take it out (after unplugging) and use it as a transistorized portable. Today, of course, most radios can also be taken out—by thieves.

The standard radio had a foot control switch mounted on the upper left portion of the floor. Without taking either hand off the wheel (or eyes off the road) the driver could change stations. Everytime the button was depressed it would go on to the next signal on the radio.

Not to be outclassed by Chevrolet or Cadillac, Oldsmobile had its gas filler concealed in the chrome panel beneath the taillight on the driver's side.

This may not be your father's Oldsmobile, but you sure as hell wish it was, don't you?

61

1957 *Chevrolet Cameo Pickup*

The Cameo was made from 1955 to 1958. Unlike most pickups of its day, the Cameo (and its counterpart the GMC Suburban) pickup had a smooth-walled carrying box with no fender well intrusion. The same look was carried over to the exterior fenders. They are smooth and straight with no tire well hump marring the lines.

62

Specifications

Overall Length	198″
Width	75⅜″
Height	74″
Weight	3,650 lbs
Wheelbase	114″
Engine	OHV V-8 283 cid/4.6 liter
Carburetor	2 bbls
Horsepower	185 @ 4,600 rpm
Bore & Stroke	3.87″ x 3″
Compression Ratio	8.5:1
Electrical	12 volt
Fuel Tank	17½ gals
Cooling System	17 qts
Tires	6.70 x 15
Suspension	front: I-beam, semielliptic leaf springs
	rear: solid axle, semielliptic leaf springs
Frame	channel section
Transmission	3-speed
	overdrive (optional)
	automatic (optional)
Rear Axle Ratio	3.7:1 manual
	4.11:1 overdrive
	3.55:1 automatic
Price	$2,300
Owner	Roger Rohde/NJ
Body Style	½-ton pickup

Accessories

Power Steering
AM Radio
E-Z Eye (Tinted) Glass
Directional Signals
Backup Lights
Chromed Bumpers and Grille
Heater/Defroster
Whitewall Tires
Windshield Washer
Day/Night Mirror
Cigarette Lighter
Two-Tone Paint

The interior walls of the carrying box were fiberglass, eliminating the rust problem. The floor was oak with metal ridges or strips running the length of the bed. The strips were raised above the wood so any cargo sliding over the floor would rest on them and not the wood while you pushed or rolled your cargo in.

The spare tire rested under the tailgate in an enclosed compartment parallel to the ground. The rear taillights look as if they are left over from the 1954 Chevy. They aren't. They are totally different, larger and more rectangular.

She shuuure is pretty!

1958 Buick Century

Mist Green—just the color of the car starts the mind on a trip off into the sunset. Add a color-matching interior and power windows/seat/steering in a convertible with some chrome, and hey, this is living!

This car has been a New York car its entire life and has no rust, dings, dents, or any other minor "infractions." The car has been well cared for by its first owner and its current owner, Bernard Minutella. Bernie sleeps in the garage and the Buick sleeps in the house.

Specifications

Overall Length	211.8" (Special/Century)
	219.1" (Super/Roadmaster)
	227" (Limited)
Width	78.1"
	79.8" (Limited)
Height	56.9"
	59.6" (Super/Roadmaster/Limited)
Weight	4,241 or 4,250 lbs
Wheelbase	122" (Special/Century)
	127.5" (Super/Roadmaster/ Limited)
Engine	OHV V-8 364 cid/6.0 liter
Carburetor	4 bbls
	2 bbls (Special)
Horsepower	300 @ 4,600 rpm
	250 @ 4,400 rpm (Special)
Bore & Stroke	4.125" x 3.4"
Compression Ratio	10.0:1
	9.5:1 (Special)
Electrical	12 volt
Fuel Tank	20 gals
Cooling System	18 qts
Tires	7.60 x 15
	8.00 x 15 (Roadmaster/Limited)
Suspension	front: ind, coil springs, ball joints
	rear: solid axle, coil springs
Frame	X-type
Transmission	automatic (Dynaflow)
Rear Axle Ratio	3.23:1
Price	$3,680
Owner	Bernard Minutella/NY
Color: Mist Green	

Accessories

Power Steering
Power Brakes
Heater/Defroster
Electric Clock
Power Windows
Transistorized Radio
Trip Odometer
Fuel, Temperature, Oil Pressure, and Amps Gauges
Power Seat
Dual Exhaust
Trunk Light/Glove Box Light
Parking Brake Warning Light
Dual Side View Mirrors

One of the options offered on the 1958 Buick was air suspension, which had a high-lift feature for deep ruts or steep ramps. In practical use the air ride was no better than the normal spring ride—and at higher expense and maintenance. It would be offered for two more years. The Dynaflow transmission was improved with three turbines instead of two for better fuel economy in city driving while providing better acceleration for highway entrance or whenever the driver wanted or needed more punch. The housing for the transmission weighed only twenty-six pounds; it was made of aluminum.

Buick offered four basic model choices in 1958: Special, Century, Super, and Roadmaster, as well as a special Roadmaster called the Limited. The Super and Roadmaster were 219 inches long while the Limited was 227 inches long. This car was BIG. It was made for one year, 1958, and was quietly put to sleep. It was too big even for Buick people. The Limited had more chrome than the other models and was distinguished by three sets of five chrome stripes alongside the rear chrome cove quarter panel.

Except for the 1958 Oldsmobile, there is probably no better example of the chrome age than a 1958 Buick. It is the embodiment of the 1950s: color, style, chrome, spirit, pizzazz.

Whether cruising on a warm summer night or parked at the town marina or among its peers at car shows, the Century is a knockout and an attention getter. If you are fortunate enough to see this particular car sometime and there is the usual crowd around it, you may wonder who the owner is and what he looks like. That will be easy. In addition to a huge grin, Bernie will be the only one who is not green . . . with envy.

1958 *Cadillac Eldorado Seville*

The Eldorado Seville was first introduced by Cadillac in 1956. Prior to that, from 1952 to 1955, the Eldorado was only available as a convertible. To differentiate one from the other, in convertible form the Eldorado was known as the Biarritz.

The Eldorado had different body styles than the standard Cadillac. Whether it was a prediction of the future or just to be different, the 1958 Eldorados had a small, straight-at-you fin. In a few years (after the magnificent

Specifications

Overall Length	223.4"
Width	80"
Height	58"
Weight	5,000 lbs
Wheelbase	129.5"
Engine	OHV V-8 365 cid/6.0 liter
Carburetor	3–2 bbls (tri-power)
Horsepower	335 @ 4,800 rpm
Bore & Stroke	4" x 3.62"
Compression Ratio	10.25:1
Electrical	12 volt
Fuel Tank	20 gals
Cooling System	18.7 qts
Tires	8.20 x 15
Suspension	front: ind, coil springs, ball joints
	rear: solid axle, coil springs
	air suspension (optional)
Frame	X-type
Transmission	automatic (Hydra-Matic)
Rear Axle Ratio	3.77:1
Price	$8,300
Owner	Dominick B. Tucci/NJ

Accessories

Power Steering
Power Brakes
Heater/Defroster
Electric Clock
Six-Way Power Seat
Remote-Controlled Outside Mirror (Driver's Side)
Power Windows Including Vent Windows
Air-Conditioning
Remote Trunk Release & Pull Down
Cruise Control
Autronic Eye (Headlight Dimmer)
Signal Seeking Radio with Rear Speaker
Power Antenna
Blower-Type Rear Window Defogger
Power Door Locks
Full-Size Spare Tire
Trip Odometer
Fog Lamps
Sabre Spoke Wheels
Gold Grille (No-Charge Option)
Fabric-Covered Roof (No-Charge Option)

fins of 1959 to 1960) the fin would get smaller and finally disappear after 1964.

The 1958 Eldorado differs from the 1957 only slightly. The 1957 had single headlights and it did not have the chrome spears or hash marks on the lower rear quarter panels. The 1957 used 2–4 bbls, and not tri-power as in 1958. All other Caddys used a single 4 bbls.

The only option on the Eldorado was air-conditioning. Everything else was standard equipment for the luxury cruiser of the 50s. The fabric-covered top was a no-charge option.

In addition to the standard power seat there was also a power memory seat that would "remember" two previously selected positions.

This was the last year of the hidden-in-the-taillight gas filler and also the last year of the glorious Dagmar/bullet bumpers. Other cars could park at ease after 1958.

If, as the expression went from the late 1930s into the 1950s, "the Cadillac of cars" exemplified luxury and quality, then the Eldorado is the Cadillac of Cadillacs!

1958 *Edsel*

Poor Edsel Ford. Say Lincoln Continental, and people think of an elegantly styled car of the 1940s with a V-12 engine. But very few people know that Edsel Ford helped plan and design that car. Say Edsel, and people think of the car named after Edsel Ford. When the 1958 Edsel made its debut in September 1957, Edsel Ford had

Specifications

Overall Length	213" (Ranger/Pacer)	218.9" (Corsair/Citation)
Width	78.9"	79.9"
Height	56.4"	56.8"
Weight	3,800 lbs	4,200 lbs
Wheelbase	118"	124.1"
Engine	OHV V-8 361 cid/5.9 liter (Ranger/Pacer)	
	OHV V-8 410 cid/6.7 liter (Corsair/Citation)	
Carburetor	4 bbls.	
Horsepower	303 @ 4,600 rpm/361 V-8	
	345 @ 4,600 rpm/410	
Bore & Stroke	4.05" x 3.50"/361 V-8	
	4.20 x 3.70"/410 V-8	
Compression Ratio	10.5:1	
Electrical	12 volt	
Fuel Tank	20 gals	
Cooling System	19.5 qts (361 V-8) 23 qts (410 V-8)	
Tires	8.00 x 14 (Ranger/Pacer) 8.50 x 14 (Corsair/Citation)	
Suspension	front: ind, coil springs	
	rear: solid axle, leaf springs	
	air suspension (optional)	
Frame	full frame, side rails	
Transmission	3-speed manual	
	overdrive (optional)	
	automatic/push button (standard on Corsair/Citation)	
Rear Axle Ratio	3.56:1 manual	
	3.70:1 overdrive	
	2.91:1 automatic	
Price	$2,600 to $3,100 (Ranger/Pacer)	
	$3,400 to $3,800 (Corsair/Citation)	
	($3,615 for this Citation)	
Owner	Bob Marconi/NY	

been dead for fourteen years. Fortunately for Edsel very few people know the car is named after him, but the name is etched on the bottom of grease pits as one of the all-time blunders of an auto company.

In the early 1950s the overall feeling at Ford Motor Company was that they needed more models. There was only Ford, Mercury, and the luxury Lincoln in the product line. Another intermediate car line was needed. By the halfway mark of model year 1955, which was a banner year for the auto industry, the thinking at Ford (and at the other automakers) was "if we only had more cars and more models we could sell those, too."

By the time 1958 came, the country and the economy had changed. There was a recession, and just how often could people keep trading in a car that was only two or three years old for a new one, especially when that not-so-old one looked and ran pretty well.

For two years before its debut, Ford kept dropping mouth-watering press releases about its "new car." When it finally made its debut, the public did not respond as Ford had hoped it would. Ford had projections of 200,000 units being sold the first year. Reality was closer to 62,000—not bad for a first-time car but not good if you hoped for 200,000.

The car had some innovative features, from self-adjusting brakes to Auto Lube, which enabled one to lube the car by just pushing a button. (The secret was to remember to keep the bowl that held the grease for the lube full and to push the button.) The Edsel also had a push-button transmission mounted in the hub of the steering wheel where it could be operated with either hand and was out of the reach of children. The push buttons were electrically operated, unlike the mechanical linkage in the Mercury and Chrysler product line, or American Motors designs.

69

Accessories

Power Steering
Power Brakes
Power Windows
Heater/Defroster
Power Seat
Air-Conditioning
Outside Mirror (Driver's Side and Passenger Side)
AM Radio
Tachometer
Remote Trunk Release
Dual Exhaust
Two-Tone Paint
Tri-Tone Paint
Seat Belts
Electric Windshield Wipers
Compass
Rear Mounted Antenna (Single or Dual)
Engine Compartment Light
Power Door Locks
Auto Lube (Push-Button Chassis Lubrication)
Windshield Washer
Tinted Glass
Spotlight

The Edsel was also priced about the same as a Mercury, but with a lot more to offer in the way of standard features, including a big V-8 on the Corsair and Citation lines. All this and the recession aside, there was the design of the car. There were the distinctive horizontal boomerang-shaped taillights. And then there was the front of the car, with its famed vertical grille, which was called everything from a horse's collar to parts of the human anatomy. In 1958 this was a strange car—a good car, but strange. By midyear plans were being made at Ford to scrap the car.

The 1959 model was built on a Ford chassis with many body and mechanical parts readily interchangeable with Ford. By 1960 the Edsel was a car in name only. It was really just a Ford with different trim. With rumors filling newspaper columns and the economy on shaky legs, 44,800 Edsels were sold in 1959 and 2,946 in 1960 when the word was out from Ford that this would be the final year.

There are many "ifs" to be said for the Edsel, which after the fact seem to make sense. But the bottom line is that Ford Motor Company expected sales of 200,000 the first year and sold only 62,000. By way of comparison, in 1958 the entire Japanese auto industry did not sell 1,500 cars in the United States. Even by 1963 this total ran to only 7,000 cars sold. Edsel sold over 100,000 cars in two years (not counting the 1960 version).

The Edsel was unique; it was a good car. There was nothing wrong with its engine or mechanical components and it was well made. But it was not an instant success in the minds of Ford Company executives and it was scrapped.

Just five years after the demise of the Edsel, Ford would have the last laugh—all the way to the bank with the Mustang.

1959 *Chevrolet Impala*

Wings—more than anything those have come to symbolize the '59 Chevy. The '59 Chevy was lower, wider, and longer than the '58 models, more like a baby Cadillac.

The Impala line was expanded to include a four-door hardtop as well as a four-door sedan, in addition to the two-door hardtop and the convertible seen here. New for 1959 was the dry-type air cleaner which, with the exception of the fuel-injected engines, replaced the oil-bath

Specifications

Overall Length	211"
Width	80"
Height	54.3"/convertible 56.3"/sedan
Weight	3,615 lbs
Wheelbase	199"
Engine	OHV V-8 348 cid/5.7 liter
	OHV V-8 283 cid/4.6 liter
	OHV Straight 6-cyl 235.5 cid/3.8 liter
Carburetor/ Horsepower	4 bbls 348 V-8 250 bhp @ 4,400 rpm
	3–2 bbls 348 V-8 (optional) 315 bhp @ 5,600 rpm
	2 bbls 282 V-8 185 bhp @ 4,600 rpm
	4 bbls 283 V-8 (optional) 220 bhp @ 4,800 rpm
	2–4 bbls 283 V-8 (optional) 270 bhp @ 6,000 rpm
	fuel injection 283 V-8 (optional) 290 bhp @ 6,200 rpm
	2 bbls 6-cyl 135 bhp @ 4,000 rpm
Bore & Stroke	4.13" x 3.25" 348 V-8
	3.87" x 3.00" 283 V-8
	3.56" x 3.93" 6-cyl
Compression Ratio	8.5:1 283 V-8/2 bbls
	9.5:1 283 V-8/4 bbls
	10.5:1 283 V-8/2–4 bbls/fuel injection
	9.5:1 348 V-8/4 bbls
	10.5:1 348 V-8/3–2 bbls
	8.25:1 6-cyl
Electrical	12 volt
Fuel Tank	20 gals
Cooling System	18 qts 6-cyl
	18½ qts 283 V-8
	22 qts 348 V-8
Tires	7.50 x 14
	8.00 x 14 convertible/station wagon
Suspension	front: ind, coil springs
	rear: solid axle, coil springs
Frame	X-type
Transmission	3-speed manual (standard)
	overdrive (optional)
	4-speed floor shift
	Powerglide/2-speed automatic (optional)
	Turboglide/3-speed automatic (optional)
Rear Axle Ratio	3.36:1 automatic
	3.55:1 manual
	4.11:1 overdrive
Price	$2,849
Owner	Roger Rohde/NJ

Accessories

Power Steering
Power Brakes
Power Windows
Power Seat
Air-Conditioning
Heater/Defroster
Seat Belts
Dry-Type Air Cleaner Except on Fuel Injection Engines
Dual Exhaust
Power Antenna
Radio with Rear Speaker (Manual and Pushbutton/Optional)
Windshield Washer
Padded Dash
Air Suspension
Positraction (Limited Slip Differential) (3.36, 3.55, or 4.11:1 Rear Axle Ratios)
Two-Tone Paint
Tinted Glass

units. Available on the fuel-injected 283 V-8 and on the 348 V-8 was the close-ratio four-speed that was used on the Corvette.

This was America's car. In countless ads in 1959, the Chevy was always displayed in some simple outdoor setting—e.g., with the Golden Gate Bridge in the background. There was a minimal amount of copy. This car did not have to be sold; people wanted to buy it!

1959 *Plymouth Fury*

For 1959 the Plymouth Fury (along with the entire Chrysler line of cars) underwent some restyling. The basic shape was still of the Forward Look, but the front and rear were updated. (The 1958 Plymouth, except for dual headlights and a small round taillight in the fin instead of a slim rectangular one, was identical to a 1957.) For 1959, the Fury was no longer limited to a two-door hardtop performance car. It was now the top of the line

Specifications

Overall Length	210"
Width	78.6"
Height	54.8" (sedan 57")
Weight	3,670 lbs
Wheelbase	118" (station wagon 122")
Engine	L-head straight 6-cyl 230 cid/3.8 Liter
	OHV V-8 318 cid/5.2 liter
	OHV V-8 361 cid/5.9 liter (dual point distributor)
Carburetor	1 bbl 6-cyl
	4 bbls 318 V-8
	4 bbls 361 V-8
Horsepower	132 @ 3,600 rpm 6-cyl
	260 @ 4,400 rpm 318 V-8
	305 @ 4,600 rpm 361 V-8
Bore & Stroke	3.25" x 4.62" 6-cyl
	3.91" x 3.31" 318 V-8
	4.12" x 3.38" 361 V-8
Compression Ratio	8.0:1 6-cyl
	9.0:1 318 V-8
	10.0:1 361 V-8
Electrical	12 volt
Fuel Tank	20 gals
Cooling System	14 qts/6 cyl 21 qts/318 V-8 17 qts/361 V-8
Tires	7.50 x 14
Suspension	front: ind, torsion bar
	rear: solid axle, leaf springs
Frame	cross member on double channel box section, side rails
Transmission	3-speed manual
	overdrive (optional)
	Power-Flite (optional on 6-cyl)
	Torque-Flite (optional on V-8)
Rear Axle Ratio	3.73:1 manual
	4.10:1 overdrive
	3.31:1 automatic
Price	$3,125
Owner	Salvatore Anicito/NJ

Accessories

Power Steering
Power Brakes
Heater/Defroster
Power Seat
Swivel Seat

with a four-door hardtop, a four-door sedan, and a two-door hardtop. The Sport Fury was the top of the Fury line with a two-door hardtop and convertible. It was available with the optional 361 cid V-8, which had a compression of 10.0:1, dual-breaker distributor, and 305 hp @ 4,600 rpm. Besides the standard 318 cid V-8, Plymouth also offered an inline 230 cid 6-cyl.

One of the big new options on the Fury and other Chrysler cars was the swivel front seat. By releasing a lever on the side of the seat, it would automatically swing outward forty degrees for ease of entry and exit. In many ads this feature was aimed directly toward women so they "could exit like a lady."

The Plymouth also offered a modified air suspension unit. It was used on the rear only and had leaf springs left in place in the event of a failure. So much for air suspension. Fuel injection, which was introduced in 1958, was not available in 1959.

Like its big brother, Imperial, the Fury offered the simulated spare look on the trunk. There was also an electronically controlled self-dimming rearview mirror. When it sensed too bright a beam from the car behind, it automatically flipped to cut glare.

Outside Mirror Driver's Side (Remote Controlled)
Outside Mirror Passenger Side
Power Windows
Air-Conditioning
AM Radio
Power Antenna
Power Door Locks
Full-Size Spare Tire
Automatic Headlight Dimmer
Electric Clock
Seat Belts
Air Suspension
Dual Exhaust
Electronically Controlled Self-Dimming Rearview Mirror

1959 *Lincoln Continental Mark IV*

T he Lincoln Continental of 1958 to 1960 was basically a luxurious version of the standard Lincoln. But was it ever luxurious—or ostentatious, if you prefer.

The main point of difference between the standard Lincoln and the Continental was the forward-sloping rear window, which was electrically controlled by the driver and went all the way down. The two-door and four-door hardtop and the convertible all had this feature.

75

These cars/land yachts were the largest unit-bodied cars ever built. Harley Copp, who was director of Lincoln engineering when these cars were made, was against the unit body, as was Paul Kuhn, Lincoln's executive engineer on the Lincoln Continental project for this series. They both felt (as many engineers do today) that on a small car unit body is fine and an advantage, but a big car should be frame-bodied. Earle MacPherson (yes, as in MacPherson strut suspension) was vice president of engineering at Ford Motor Company, and he liked the idea of a unit body. It was an all-new car (in 1958) and Earle and Lew Crusoe, who was ex-vice president for Ford car and truck, wanted to make a statement with this all-new series of Lincoln, and unit body won out. Or, more simply, "the boss over the engineer."

Any advantage of a unit body is lost on a large (over 3,400-lb car.) This was, and still is, a basic philosophy of car engineers on car body/frame design. The thousands of spot welds do not enhance the overall construction of the car and do not make it better than a body on frame construction. Simply put, there is nothing like a good solid chassis to support the body of a large car.

The next step after the unit-body decision was the type of suspension. Connie Reuter, who was in charge of design for ride and handling on the Lincoln of 1958 to 1960, wanted to go with a conventional SLA (short and long arm) suspension with coil springs front and rear. He and several other people felt that on a car so large MacPherson strut would not be any advantage and possibly could be detrimental. When this subject was brought up at a design meeting, Mr. MacPherson agreed and went right along with the conventional system.

There was then some discussion on an air ride suspension as an option. After much testing, it was decided that air suspension was more hot air than anything

else, and this option was never offered on the Lincoln. In 1960 the rear coil springs were changed to leaf springs, which gave a slightly more rigid ride.

All these decisions were not made in 1958 but in 1955, so there would be enough time to tool up for this car. Because of the boom year 1955 (over 9,000,000 American cars sold), the engineers and auto industry executives planned the 1958 models toward the excess side. If the 1955 models were doing so well, it would follow that more would be better. No one planned on the "Eisenhower recession." By 1958 and 1959 big car sales had hit the skids.

As for that unit body, because of it the Lincoln could sit four people across as opposed to three and a half in an Imperial or Cadillac. The transmission hump was well concealed beneath the floor and the flat roof had plenty of

Specifications

Overall Length	227"
Width	80.1"
Height	56.8"
Weight	5,256 lbs
Wheelbase	131"
Engine	OHV V-8 430/7.0 liter
Carburetor	4 bbls
Horsepower	350 @ 4,400 rpm
Bore & Stroke	4.30" x 3.70"
Compression Ratio	10.0:1
Electrical	12 volt
Fuel Tank	23 gals
Cooling System	23 qts
Tires	9.50 x 14
Suspension	front: ind, coil springs
	rear: solid axle, coil springs
Frame	unit body
Transmission	automatic (Turbo-Drive)
Rear Axle Ratio	2.89:1
Price	$7,100
Owner	Melvyn Lipschitz/NY

Accessories

Power Steering
Power Brakes
Heater/Defroster
Electric Clock
Six-Way Power Seat
Remote-Controlled Side Mirror (Driver's Side)
Power Windows (Including Vent Windows and Power Rear Window)
Air-Conditioning
Remote Trunk Release
Cruise Control
Automatic Headlight Dimmer
Radio with FM Converter
Power Antenna
Power Door Locks
Fuel, Oil, Amps, and Temperature Gauges
Automatic Multilube

headroom. The ride was slightly harsh compared to a Cadillac or Imperial. As for cornering, the Lincoln was superb.

The car could go from 0–60 in 8.7 seconds, with a top speed of 125 mph. A 1959 Mercedes 190SL, a so-called sports car, went from 0–60 in 13.2 seconds and had a top speed of 106 mph. The Lincoln weighed 5,200 lbs, could hold six people very comfortably, had every convenience offered today except for a computer, while the 190SL weighed 2,500 lbs, sat two people with some comfort, and offered roll-up windows and an adequate heater at a cost of $5,000.

The magnificent Mark IV is a tank! There are no rattles, squeaks, or vibrations. That big, solid 430/V-8 propels this car onto highways effortlessly, and purrs like a kitten when just standing still or cruising down a country lane. As quick as the 1959 Continental was, it was a detuned version of the 430/V-8 that appeared in 1958. That engine had an output of 375 @ 4,800 rpm. The 1958 Mark III also had bullet bumpers, which the 1959 did not, resulting in two inches less overall length. (These bumpers reappeared on the 1960 Mark V.)

Whatever the backroom bickering that went on from 1954 to 1956, on the final body/frame design of this land yacht, it works! The car you see here is a totally original car. The interior, exterior, chrome, and engine have never been touched. Aside from normal maintenance (oil change, tune-up, etc., but no lube job for this car is self-lubricating), the engine has never been touched or rebuilt —or needed to.

In an ad for the 1959 Mark IV, a red convertible is shown with a quote from Ralph Waldo Emerson: "Nothing is more simple than greatness," to which should be added the line by one of the preeminent car authorities today, Fred Kanter: "Nothing is more great than ostentatiousness!"

1959 *Pontiac Bonneville*

Wide track—that was the word for Pontiac in 1959. The front and rear tread were increased by five inches. Combined with the lower center of gravity over the previous year, it made for a vast improvement in ride and stability.

For passenger comfort in the rear there was a duct to direct hot (or cold if the car had air-conditioning) air there. In 1959 the car was praised for the restraint designers exercised in their use of chrome and trim.

In an ad illustrating a man getting into his new Pontiac driven by his wife at a hotel, the copy goes, "Men,

Specifications

Overall Length	221" 213" (Catalina)
Width	81"
Height	54" (conv/2-door)
	54.5" (4-door)
	56" (sedan)
Weight	4,100 lbs
Wheelbase	124" 122" (Catalina)
Engine	OHV V-8 389 V-8/6.3 liter
Carburetor	4 bbls
	3–2 bbls (optional)
Horsepower	300 @ 4,600 rpm 4 bbls
	345 @ 4,800 rpm 3–2 bbls
Bore & Stroke	4.06" x 3.75"
Compression Ratio	10.0:1 Hydra-Matic
	8.6:1 manual
Electrical	12 volt
Fuel Tank	20 gals
Cooling System	22½ qts
Tires	8.50 x 14 (station wagon/ convertible)
	8.00 x 14 (all other models)
Suspension	front: ind, coil springs
	rear: solid axle, coil springs
Frame	X-type with tubular center
Transmission	3-speed manual
	Hydra-Matic (optional)
Rear Axle Ratio	3.42:1 manual
	3.23:1 automatic
Price	$3,550
Owner	Ann & Donald LoFranco/NJ

Accessories

Power Steering
Power Brakes
Power Windows
Leather Interior (Standard on Bonneville Convertible)
Radio with Rear Speaker
Sportable Radio (Can Take with You)
Air-Conditioning
Windshield Washer
Two-Tone Paint
Bucket Seats
Seat Belts (Front and Rear Seats)
Tissue Dispenser
Padded Dash
Power Antenna
Tinted Glass
Heater/Defroster
Clear Plastic Seat Covers
Continental Kit
Dual Exhaust

if you'd like to turn up the flame of romance at your house, borrow a bright new Pontiac from one of our dealers tomorrow.

"Take it home, see how she looks AT it and IN it. See how she loves the solid security of Wide-Track Wheels. See how she loves you for being so intelligently thoughtful. Of course she'll want to go back to the dealer's with you to help choose colors and fabrics. Give her this privilege. It's well worth it."

Some things do change for the better in time, but that Pontiac still looks better than anything coming down the road today. As for that flame of romance, if you ever see Don LoFranco in this car, ask him; better yet, ask his wife Ann—she bought the car!

1959 *Cadillac Coupe de Ville*

Fins. In 1948 Cadillac had a gently sloping upward bump on the rear fenders. Some people called it a fin. It was supposedly styled after the tail of a P-38 fighter plane of World War II. In 1959 Cadillac took the fin a little further. (In 1960 the bulletlike taillights were removed on the sharklike fin and a slim taillight was installed in their place, in addition to a taillight in the chrome housing, beneath the fin.)

Style aside for a moment, the cars are tanks. The ride and quality are outstanding, the engine a refined pow-

erhouse. In addition to the car's trunk and exterior space there was interior space, "a real make-out parlor."

There were some "auto experts" back when this car was new who ridiculed it, as some do even to this day. But the fortunate few who still own one or more (as I do) are laughing all the way to the bank. This car was all iron and steel; the only plastic on it was the taillight lenses. The only items not available on this Caddy were an FM radio, tape deck or CD, and a computer.

The car may be outrageous, but at least the price wasn't. And how many cars today have songs written about them? My pink Mercedes Benz? Nooo way!

Specifications

Overall Length	225"
Width	80.1"
Height	54.1" (conv/2-door/4-window)
	56.2" (Fleetwood)
Weight	4,900 lbs
Wheelbase	130"
Engine	OHV V-8 390 cid/6.4 liter
Carburetor	4 bbls
	3–2 bbls/Eldorado
Horsepower	325 @ 4,800 rpm 4 bbls
	345 @ 4,800 rpm 3–2 bbls
Bore & Stroke	4" x 3.87"
Compression Ratio	10.5:1
Electrical	12 volt
Fuel Tank	21 gals
Cooling System	19.25 qts
Tires	8.20 x 15
Suspension	front: ind, coil springs
	rear: solid axle, coil springs
	air suspension (optional)
Frame	X-type
Transmission	Hydra-Matic (4-speed automatic)
Rear Axle Ratio	3.07:1
Price	$5,270
Owner	Wade Jacobs/NY

Accessories

Power Steering (Standard)
Power Brakes (Standard)
Power Windows (Standard)
Heater/Defroster (Standard)
Electric Clock (Standard)
Two-Way Power Seat (Standard)
Six-Way Power Seat (Optional)
Remote-Controlled Mirror Driver's Side (Standard)
Power Vent Windows
Air-Conditioning
Leather Interior
Remote Trunk Release and Pull Down
Cruise Control
Autronic Eye (Headlight Dimmer)
Signal-seeking Radio with Rear Speaker (Standard)
Power Antenna (Standard)
Blower-Type Rear Window Defogger
Power Door Locks
Trip Odometer
Air Suspension (Standard on Eldorado/Fleetwood 60)
Bucket Seats
Fog Lights
Sabre Spoke Wheels
Dual 90s/General Tire Co. Puncture-Proof Tire, $100 Each
Dual Exhaust (Standard)

1960 *Buick Electra 225*

The 1960 Buick is similar in profile but radically different than its predecessor, the 1959, which in turn was a radical change from the 1958 Buick.

The headlights, which are now horizontal, were on a forty-five-degree angle in 1959. The lines and angles on the 1959 were all razor sharp. In 1960 those edges got a curve or roundness to them. Missing for 1958 and 1959, the portholes were once again brought back onto the front fender.

There were three model lines: the LeSabre, Invicta, and Electra, which had a series unto itself called the

Specifications

Overall Length	218" (LeSabre/Invicta)
	221.3" (Electra)
	225" (Electra 225)
Width	80"
Height	54.4" (convertible) 57.1" (sedan)
Weight	4,650 lbs
Wheelbase	123" (LeSabre/Invicta)
	126" (Electra/Electra 225)
Engine	OHV V-8 401 cid/6.5 liter
	OHV V-8 364 cid/6.0 liter
	(LeSabre)
Carburetor	4 bbls 401 V-8
	2 bbls 364 V-8
Horsepower	250 @ 4,400 rpm 364 V-8
	325 @ 4,400 rpm 401 V-8
Bore & Stroke	4.1875" x 3.64" 401 V-8
	4.125" x 3.40" 364 V-8
Compression Ratio	10.25:1 364 V-8/401 V-8
Electrical	12 volt
Fuel Tank	20 gals
Cooling System	18.5 qts
Tires	8.00 x 15
Suspension	front: ind, coil springs
	rear: solid axle, coil springs
Frame	X-type
Transmission	automatic (Twin Turbine)
Rear Axle Ratio	3.21:1
Price	$4,192
Owner	Gary Rabinowitz/NY

Accessories

Power Steering (Standard)
Power Brakes (Standard)
Heater/Defroster (Standard)
Power Seat (Standard)
Power Windows (Standard)
Air-Conditioning
Power Antenna
Radio
Automatic Headlight Dimmer
Tinted Glass (Standard)
Electric Clock (Standard)
Cruise Control
Power Vent Windows
Dual Exhaust
Windshield Washer (Standard)

Leather Interior (Standard)
Trip Odometer (Standard)
Air Suspension
Bucket Seats

Electra 225. It was an ultra-luxurious model which was distinguished from the standard Electra by its stainless steel lower molding running the length of the car. The 225 was also four inches longer than the Electra.

The LeSabre series used the 364 cid V-8 and had a wheelbase of 123 inches. The Invicta series shared the same wheelbase but had the 401 V-8 as its powerplant, the same engine used in the Electra and Electra 225.

The silky smooth ride and whisper quiet motor belie the fact that this car can perform, whether that be on the road or when parked with someone special overlooking a lake.

Gary, the owner of this 225, was nice enough to let me drive the car to the location where it was to be photographed. His son Adam came along with me while Gary followed in his 1953 Buick. The temptation to give the car some throttle while driving was too much, and much to Gary's regret and his son Adam's delight, I did.

As much as Adam likes this car, his favorite (and one he plans on getting) is the 1958 Edsel. As we were coming to a stoplight, Adam and I were talking about cars and the Edsel and Buick in particular, when suddenly Adam said, "Toyotas don't have whitewalls." When you think about it, a Toyota with wide whites is ludicrous. When you think about it some more and then look at the 225 convertible, whitewalls aren't the only thing Toyotas are lacking.

Adam and his father get along great due to the fact there is not that wide a gap in their ages—at five, Adam is only slightly younger than Gary.

1960 *Pontiac Bonneville*

The 1960 Pontiac was restyled to a small degree. The basic shape was the same as the 1959 but with a new grille and rear end treatment. The taillights were similar to those on the 1958 Pontiacs.

There was even more restraint in the use of chrome and exterior trim. The lines of the car were standing more on their own. Wide-Track was still emphasized in ads for the car. The Bonneville continued to be the top of the line with its two- and four-door hardtop, the sporty

Specifications

Overall Length	220.7″ Bonneville/Star Chief
	213″ Catalina/Ventura
Width	80.7″
Height	54.8″ 2-door/4-door hardtop
	56.6″ sedan
	54.2″ convertible
Weight	4,100 lbs
Wheelbase	124″ Bonneville/Star Chief
	122″ Catalina/Ventura
Engine	OHV V-8 389 cid/6.3 liter
Carburetor	2 bbls Catalina/Ventura/Star Chief
	4 bbls Bonneville
	3–2 bbls (optional all models)
Horsepower	283 @ 4,400 rpm 2 bbls
	303 @ 4,600 rpm 4 bbls
Bore & Stroke	4.06″ x 3.75″
Compression Ratio	10.25:1 automatic
	8.60:1 manual
Electrical	12 volt
Fuel Tank	20 gal
Cooling System	22½ qts
Tires	8.00 x 14
	8.50 x 14 station wagon and all
	cars with a/c
Suspension	front: ind, coil springs
	rear: solid axle, coil springs
Frame	X-type with tubular center
Transmission	3-speed manual
	4-speed floor shift (midyear
	option)
	Hydra-Matic (optional)
Rear Axle Ratio	3.42:1 manual
	3.23:1 automatic
Price	$4,150
Owner	George Coppola/NJ

convertible, and the four-door Safari wagon—all introduced in 1959.

In an ad showing the Bonneville beside a pool in a sunny Florida-type setting, some of the copy reads: "Don't dream—drive! That's what a new car seems to urge." With this '60 Bonny you could do both. It is a dream machine, and anything is possible.

Accessories

Power Steering
Power Brakes
Power Windows
Power Seat
Power Antenna
Radio with Wonder Bar and Push Buttons
Sportable Radio (Two Knobs Only, But Can Take with You)
Air-Conditioning
Leather Interior (Standard on Bonneville Convertible)
Windshield Washer
Two-Tone Paint
Bucket Seats
Seat Belts
Padded Dash
Tinted Glass
Dual Exhaust
Heater/Defroster
Continental Kit
Remote-Controlled Driver's Mirror
Under-Hood Light

1961 *Oldsmobile Starfire*

For 1961 the entire Oldsmobile line got new frames, new front and rear suspension, a new automatic transmission, and new bodies.

The new body style was shorter by 6.5 inches in the 88 series and 3 inches in the 98. Overall width was reduced by 3.8 inches in both the 88 and 98, with no reduction in interior space.

The windshield is entirely new, replacing the wraparound with the dog leg that got more than one person in the knee.

The Starfire was an entirely new series and only

Specifications

Overall Length	212" (Starfire/88) 218" (98)
Width	77.2"
Height	54.5" (convertible/2-door hardtop)
	56.5" (sedan)
Weight	4,300 lbs
Wheelbase	123" (Starfire/88) 126" (98)
Engine	OHV V-8 394 cid/6.4 liter)
Carburetor	2 bbls 88
	4 bbls (Starfire/98)
Horsepower	330 @ 4,600 rpm (Starfire)
	325 @ 4,600 rpm (98)
	250 @ 4,400 rpm (88)
Bore & Stroke	4.125" x 3.688"
Compression Ratio	10.25:1 (Starfire)
	10.00:1 (98)
	8.75.1 (88)
Electrical	12 volt
Fuel Tank	20 gals
Cooling System	20¼ qts
Tires	8.00 x 14 (88)
	8.50 x 14 (Starfire) 9.50 x 14 (98)
Suspension	front: ind, coil springs
	rear: solid axle, coil springs
Frame	box section
Transmission	Hydra-Matic (slim jim) *
	3-speed manual (standard on 88)
Rear Axle Ratio	3.42:1 manual
	2.87:1 automatic (88)
	3.23:1 automatic (Starfire/98)
Price	$5,139
Owner	Herbert Glaser/NJ

Accessories

Power Steering
Power Brakes
Power Windows
Bucket Seats (Standard/Power)
Tachometer
Dual Exhaust
Console
Brushed Aluminum Side Panels (Starfire)
Signal-Seeking Radio
Air-Conditioning
Heater/Defroster
Rear Window Defogger (Not Available on Convertible)

Power Antenna
Remote Trunk Release
Power Seats
Remote-Controlled Outside Mirror (Driver's Side)
Fender Skirts
Padded Dash
Windshield Washer
Leather Interior
Power Door Locks
Seat Belts

*Term used by parts suppliers to identify a special kind of Hydra-Matic with internal parts different from those used by Cadillac.

available as a convertible. It was targeted for the "personal luxury category"; it came with bucket seats, which were covered in leather. On the floor there were stainless steel rub plates, the side panels were brushed aluminum, and along the side of the car, almost from bumper to bumper, there was brushed aluminum molding. Power windows, power brakes, power steering, tachometer, and the center console were all standard on this car.

If the 1950s were known for fins, chrome, multi-colored cars, and multiangled fenders, the early 60s were a show in clean, simple lines, with sharp restraint in the use of chrome.

The last bit of 1950s design was still on the cars of model year 1961: the wide whitewall, which by now was down to 2¼ inches in width. In 1962 it would be offered no more (by new car dealers, that is; you could always purchase them at an independent tire dealer). From 1962 on, the whitewall would be more of a white band from 1 to 1½ inches in diameter, with black rubber on either side.

1962 Pontiac Grand Prix

This was the first year for the Grand Prix. It was only available as a two-door hardtop and was featured as a "two-door sports coupe." It was basically a Pontiac Catalina with different exterior trim and grille and a sporty interior: bucket seats and center console.

89

Specifications

Overall Length	211.6″
Width	78.6″
Height	54.5″
Weight	4,000 lbs
Wheelbase	120″
Engine	OHV V-8 389 cid/6.3 liter
Carburetor	4 bbls
	3–2 bbls (optional)
Horsepower	303 @ 4,600 rpm 4 bbls
	318 @ 4,600 rpm 3–2 bbls
	333 @ 4,800 rpm 4 bbls (10.75 compression ratio)
	348 @ 4,800 rpm 3–2 bbls (10.75 compression ratio)
Bore & Stroke	4.00″ x 3.75″
Compression Ratio	10.25:1
	10.75:1 (optional)
Electrical	12 volt
Fuel Tank	25 gals
Cooling System	19½ qts
Tires	8.00 x 14
Suspension	front: ind, coil springs, ball joints, torsion action front stabilizer bar rear: solid axle, coil springs
Frame	Perimeter with box section structure, five cross members. Entire passenger section encircled by steel side members
Transmission	3-speed manual
	Hydra-Matic (slim jim/optional)
	4-speed floor shift (optional)
Rear Axle Ratio	3.23:1 (3.42:1, 3.64:1, 3.9:1, and 4.89:1/optional)
Price	$3,424.75
Owner	Martin Daniels/NY

Accessories

Power Steering
Power Brakes
Power Windows
Power Seat
Heater/Defroster (Optional)
8-Lug Aluminum Wheels (Optional)
AM Radio
Electric Clock
Tinted Glass

Remote-Controlled Outside Mirror (Driver's Side)
Air-Conditioning
Remote Trunk Release
Cruise Control
Power Antenna
Tachometer
Automatic Headlight Dimmer
Windshield Washer
Dual Exhaust (Standard)

The 1961 model year saw a new, clean, more sedate type of motor vehicle, which carried over into 1962. The Grand Prix is a crisp, let-the-lines-speak-for-the-car design. Chrome was used in moderation, and a mark of the 50s was gone—wide whites, whitewall tires that began at the inner rim and extended from 2¼ to 3 inches.

The 1962 Grand Prix here was purchased on April 6, 1962, by its original and only owner, Marty Daniels. Among some of the car's options (and prices) are: rear speaker, $14.15, backup lights, $14.31, and Saf-T-Track, $42.50. This last item is similar to the ABS (antilock braking system) on some new cars.

Today the car is used more on nice spring and summer days than in the winter, for Marty has definitely decided never to sell it. As Marty says, "When it was new, people admired it. After several years it was just an older car, and some friends asked why I didn't trade it in for a newer model. Now that it is over twenty-five years old, people tell me, 'really looks great,' or 'I had a car like that.'"

When the flowers start to bloom and the birds are chirping in the trees, Marty's words best sum up what cars of this era mean: "I can't wait to get on the road again."

1963 *Corvette Stingray*
1967 *Corvette 427*

1963 Corvette Stingray

B last off! Rocket booster at full throttle. This is the 1963 split window coupe. The car looks like it is going 150 mph just sitting at a stop sign. Here was a missile for two on wheels! 0–60 mph in 5.9 seconds and 0–100 mph in 16.5 seconds!

But forget those numbers; just look at the car, that unique rear window. It would be for 1963 only. The following year it would be one-piece, for "better visibility." The window is so sloping that taking away the split really does not help visibility at all. It just made the 1963 more desirable.

This car was not your tweed-jacket, brown-oxford-shoes, fleshy-jowled, pipe-smoking driver's car. It was a tight-T-shirt, black-leather-boots-and-jacket, blast-off-to-the-sky, the-world-is-mine car!

The Stingray as it looks here was made from 1963 to 1967. In 1968 it received some restyling and the fastback coupe was gone.

In 1965 a 396 V-8 was added as an option, and in 1966 the monster big block 427 cid V-8 appeared. There

1963 *Corvette Stingray*
Specifications

Overall Length	175"
Width	70"
Height	51"
Weight	2,870 lbs
Wheelbase	98"
Engine	OHV V-8 327 cid/5.3 liter
Carburetor	4 bbls.
	fuel injection (optional)
Horsepower	250 @ 4,400 rpm
	300 @ 5,000 rpm (optional)
	340 @ 6,000 rpm (optional)
	360 @ 6,000 rpm (optional/fuel injection)
Bore & Stroke	4.00" x 3.25"
Compression Ratio	10.50:1
	11.25:1 (optional on 340 hp and 360 hp)
Electrical	12 volt
Fuel Tank	20 gals
Cooling System	16½ qts
Tires	6.70 x 15
Suspension	front: ind, coil springs
	rear: ind, transverse leaf spring
Frame	ladder type with five cross members
Transmission	3-speed manual floor shift
	4-speed manual floor shift (optional)
	automatic floor shift (optional)
Rear Axle Ratio	3.36:1 3-speed and automatic
	3.70:1 4-speed
	3.08:1, 3.55:1, 4.11:1, and 4.56:1 (optional on 4-speed)
Price	$4,250/coupe
	$4,050/convertible
Owner	Roger Rohde/NJ

Accessories

Dual Exhaust (Standard)
Tachometer (Standard)
Clock (Standard)
Heater/Defroster (Standard)
Power Steering (Optional)
Power Brakes (Optional)
Heavy-Duty Brakes with Metallic Facings (Optional)
Air-Conditioning (Optional)
Signal-Seeking AM Radio (Optional)
AM/FM Radio (Optional)
Sebring Silver Paint (Optional) (Color of Car Shown in Photo)
Aluminum Knock-off Wheels (Optional)
Tinted Glass (Optional)
Leather Seats (Optional)
Detachable Hardtop for Convertible (Optional)
Wood-Grain Steering Wheel (Optional)
Positraction Rear Axle (Limited Slip Differential) (Optional)
Windshield Washer (Standard)
Seat Belts (Standard)
Outside Rearview Mirror (Standard)
327 V-8 Engine with 250 hp (Standard)
327 V-8 with 300 hp (Optional)
327 V-8 with 340 hp (Optional)
327 V-8 with Fuel Injection, 360 HP (Optional)
0–60 in 5.8 seconds with fuel injection
½ mile in 14.5 seconds/102 mph

were only two Stingrays, the coupe and the convertible. Put a 427 V-8 under the hood of a 1967 yellow convertible and the car is simply the best sports car in the world! 0–60 mph in 4.8 seconds, the standing quarter mile in 12.8 seconds at 112 mph. No computer chips, electronic wizardry, or digital display dash. Just a big block with 3–2 bbls, some gauges on the dash, and lots of macho. As a friend puts it: "You ever hear some people describe some restaurants with their fancy flowers, the waiters in tuxedos, the type of place you need a tie and jacket and women in evening attire? I ask how the food is. The food, that's what counts. Or you see some sophisticated lady in

93

1967 Corvette 427
Specifications

Overall Length	175"
Width	70"
Height	50"
Weight	3,050 lbs
Wheelbase	98"
Engine	OHV V-8 327 cid/5.3 liter
	OHV V-8 427 cid/7.0 liter
Carburetor	4 bbls 327 V-8
	4 bbls 427 V-8
	3–2 bbls 427 V-8
Horsepower	300 @ 5,000 rpm 327 V-8
	400 @ 5,400 rpm 427 V-8 4 bbls
	(optional)
	435 @ 5,800 rpm 427 V-8 3–2 bbls
	(optional)
Bore & Stroke	4.001" x 3.25" 327 V-8
	4.25" x 3.76" 427 V-8
Compression Ratio	10.50:1 327 V-8
	10.25:1 427 V-8 (4 bbls)
	11.00:1 427 V-8 (3–2 bbls)
Electrical	12 volt
Fuel Tank	20 gals
Cooling System	23 qts (427 V-8)
	16 qts (327 V-8)
Tires	7.75 x 15
Suspension	front: ind, coil springs
	rear: ind, transverse leaf spring
Frame	ladder type with five cross
	members
Transmission	3-speed manual floor shift
	4-speed manual floor shift
	(optional)
	automatic floor shift (optional)
Rear Axle Ratio	3.36:1 3-speed and automatic
	3.70:1 4-speed
	3.08:1, 3.55:1, 4.11:1, and 4.56:1
	(optional on 4-speed)
Price	$4,900
Owner	Roger Rohde/NJ

(427/435 bhp V-8 0–60 mph in 5.4 seconds/3.36:1 axle ratio)
(427/435 bhp V-8 0–60 mph in 4.8 seconds/4.11:1 axle ratio)
(top speed/150 mph)

Accessories

Power Steering (Optional)
Power Brakes (Optional)
Power Windows (Optional)
Air-Conditioning (Optional)
Shoulder Belts (Optional)
Tinted Windows & Tinted Windshield (Optional)
AM/FM Radio with Rear Mounted Antenna (Optional)
Heater/Defroster (Standard)
Leather Seats (Optional)
Detachable Hardtop for Convertible
Transister Ignition System (Optional)
Telescopic Steering Wheel (Optional)
Side Mount Exhaust (Optional)
Aluminum Wheels (Optional)
Positraction Rear Axle (Optional)
Wood Grain Steering Wheel (Optional)
Seat Belts (Standard)
Dual Exhaust (Standard)
Tachometer (Standard)
Windshield Washer (Standard)
Four-Wheel Disc Brakes (Optional)

her jewels and designer gown, who cares...does she screw? Yeah, I asked that of some lady I met at a party once.

"Look when you take away the fine linen, is the table really clean and is the food good? Hell, women don't go out with men for their fine intellect only. Just look at me. The Stingray with that 427 can screw...and that's what it's all about."

1964 *Buick Riviera*

I f it were not for the Thunderbird, the Riviera would probably not exist. Sales of the Thunderbird were growing each year and by 1960 sales for that year totaled almost 93,000. This was alarming news to people at GM—in particular, Bill Mitchell, styling chief at GM.

There was a crash course in what to do and how to counter the T-Bird. At first it was thought that Cadillac should introduce a personal-type car. But Cadillac sales were strong. The thinking at Cadillac was that they did not need a new model. Chevrolet was out, for the car had to have an upscale image. Buick sales had shown the most decline since 1955, and so it was decided to give Buick this

95

Specifications

Overall Length	208″
Width	76.6″
Height	53.2″
Weight	4,025 lbs
Wheelbase	117″
Engine	OHV V-8 425 cid/7.0 liter
Carburetor	4 bbls
	2–4 bbls (optional)
Horsepower	340 @ 440 rpm/4 bbls
	360 @ 4,400 rpm/2–4 bbls
Bore & Stroke	4.3125″ x 3.64″
Compression Ratio	10.25:1
Electrical	12 volt
Fuel Tank	20 gals
Cooling System	18½ qts
Tires	7.10 x 15
Suspension	front: ind, coil springs
	rear: solid axle, coil springs
Frame	Cruciform-box section, three cross members, all steel
Transmission	automatic (Turbo 400)
Rear Axle Ratio	3.23:1
Price	$4,385
Owner	Lawrence F. Insetta/NY

new marque. The original name that Bill Mitchell had in mind was LaSalle, after the Cadillac LaSalle of the 1930s. Since this was now going to be a Buick project that name was out. The first Buick hardtop in 1949 was called a Riviera, and that name was decided on for this new car.

Bill Mitchell had designed the trend-setting 1938 Cadillac 60 Special. He had always favored sharply defined angles and sheer lines. He incorporated that thinking into the Riviera, and working along with GM Special Projects Director Ned Nickles, a full-sized fiberglass model was made and the Riviera was on its way.

In 1961 Thunderbird came out with a new look. It was soft and round, unlike the square-bird look of 1958 to 1960. By 1963 the round-bird look was three years old when Buick introduced their Riviera. The car was heavily advertised, but production was limited to 40,000 to assure

Accessories

Power Steering
Power Brakes
Power Windows
Power Seat
Air-Conditioning
Heater/Defroster
Rear Window Defogger
Leather Interior
Sealt Belts
AM/FM Radio with Rear Speaker
Cornering Lights
Automatic Headlight Dimmer
Remote Trunk Release
Cruise Control
Power Door Locks
Bucket Seats (Standard)
Compass
Tissue Dispenser
Fuel, Oil, Amps, and Temperature Gauges
Tachometer
Spoke Hubcaps
Remote-Controlled Outside Mirror
Power Antenna

that demand would be greater than supply if the public liked the car.

The car you see here is a result of all this preparation by GM and Bill Mitchell. The car was recognized as a classic in design as soon as it was introduced.

It was a personal luxury car with performance. The 425/V-8 could be ordered with the optional dual quads which gave this car a top speed of 130+ mph. It was quick off the line (0–60 in 8.1 seconds) and rode like a dream. The 1963 and '64 Riviera are identical except for the 425/V-8 used in 1964. In 1963 the Riviera used a 401/V-8. With its bucket seats and center console with transmission selector mounted in it, the interior of the 1964 had the feel of a personal rocket ship. With its amber parking lights mounted into the front fenders the outside of the car has the look of a spaceship from another planet—a very beautiful spaceship. The Riviera had a look of power, stability, and elegance.

In 1963 Thunderbird sold 63,000 and the Riviera sold all 40,000 units produced. It was only offered in the two-door hardtop version, while Thunderbird had a hardtop and convertible, although after 1966 production of the Thunderbird convertible ceased. In 1964 Riviera sold 38,000 cars.

1964 *Pontiac* GTO

In early 1963, Pete Estes, general manager of the Pontiac Division, and John DeLorean, the chief engineer, decided that Pontiac should make a factory hot rod. This was still a time when car people—people who truly got a thrill from building and driving a car—worked in the auto industry, before the "marketing people" came to power. The car Pete and John wanted should also be priced under $3,000 so that young people could enjoy it and afford it.

General Motors executives had a new company policy in 1963 banning all divisions from racing activities. Pete Estes got around this by making the GTO an option

1964 *Pontiac* GTO (2-Door *Convertible*)
Specifications

Overall Length	203″
Width	73.3″
Height	53.6″
Weight	3,422 lbs
Wheelbase	115″
Engine	OHV V-8 389 cid/6.3 liter
Carburetor	3–2 bbls (optional)
	4 bbls
Horsepower	348 @ 4,000 rpm/3–2 bbls (optional)
	325 @ 4,800 rpm/4bbls
Bore & Stroke	4.06″ x 3.75″
Compression Ratio	10.75:1
Electrical	12 volt
Fuel Tank	21½ gals
Cooling System	20 qts
Tires	7.50 x 14
Suspension	front: ind, coil springs
	rear: solid axle, coil springs
Frame	full-length frame with rubber isolated body
Transmission	3-speed manul floor shift
	4-speed wide ratio floor shift (optional)
	automatic (optional)
Rear Axle Ratio	3.55:1
	(3.90:1/3.21:1/3.08:1 (optional)
Price	$3,500
Owner	Tom Stein/NY

quarter mile in 14.1 seconds/104 mph
(no computer chips or electronics)

1964 *Pontiac* GTO (2-Door *Hardtop*)
Specifications

Overall Length	203″
Width	73.3″
Height	53″
Weight	3,200 lbs
Wheelbase	115″
Engine	OHV V-8 389 cid/6.3 liter
Carburetor	4 bbls
	3–2 bbls (optional)
Horsepower	348 @ 4,900 rpm/3–2 bbls (optional)
	325 @ 4,800 rpm/4 bbls
Bore & Stroke	4.06″ x 3.75″
Compression Ratio	10.25:1
Electrical	12 volt
Fuel Tank	21½ gals
Cooling System	20 qts
Tires	7.50 x 14
Suspension	front: ind, coil springs
	rear: solid axle, coil springs
Frame	full-length frame with rubber isolated body
Transmission	3-speed manual floor shift
	4-speed wide ratio floor shift (optional)
	automatic (optional)
Rear Axle Ratio	3.55:1
	3.90:1/3.21:1 and 3.08:1 (optional)
Price	$3,200
Owner	Fred Viohl/NY

(0–60 mph in 6.9 seconds (4 bbls); quarter mile in 15 seconds/91 mph; top speed 130 mph)

package, not a model line. The first year 32,450 GTOs were sold—six times what was projected for this model.

The car was offered in a two-door sedan, two-door hardtop, and convertible. The 389 cid V-8 was offered with a 4 bbls, which was standard setup. Tri-power was an option.

This was the car that put the word "muscle" in

Accessories

Power Steering
Power Brakes
Heater/Defroster
Power Seat
Remote-Controlled Mirror Driver's Side
Power Windows
Air-Conditioning
Remote Trunk Release
AM Radio
Tilt Wheel
Fuel, Oil, Amps, and Temperature Gauges
Tachometer
Electrical Clock
Tinted Glass
Transistorized Ignition

muscle car. It could go from 0–60 in 5.7 seconds, had a top speed of 145 mph, and yet when riding on the highway or some country road was as mild as a kitten—until the pedal was put to the metal. With its special heavy-duty suspension, this car could hold its own against anything on the road. As a comparison, a 1963 Porsche 356A/1600 GS sold for $4,400, went from 0–60 in 11.5 seconds, and had a top speed of 124 mph. It held two people and a pastrami sandwich, had terrible ventilation—hot in summer, cold in winter—and was dangerous on anything but a dry road.

The GTO was the basic Pontiac Tempest, except for the performance engine and slightly different trim. (Note the blacked-out grille, GTO letters, and air scoops on the hood.)

The Tempest for model year 1961–1963 had independent suspension and a transaxle—the transmission was in the rear. For 1964 the Tempest went back to the conventional system of independent front and solid rear axle.

The term GTO (popularly known as "goat") really stands for Gran Turismo Omolgato. Many European auto-makers put this term on their high-price, high-performance cars. The GTO was high performance, but not high priced.

As for upsetting some Porsche owners and some "car experts" on the Porsche/GTO comparison, I owned them both. The Porsche is long gone, the Pontiac I still have and will have for a long, long time.

1964 *Thunderbird*

A n American original—from the day the first two-seat Thunderbird came gliding down Main Street, U.S.A., people knew this was an American car. From the ease of its automatic controls to its understated performance, this was *the* car. It had one pure American trait that many cars have been searching for ever since—a spirit of gaiety, of the joy of living: fun, fun, fun!

As you can see by looking at the 1964 Thunderbird, it has changed some from that first one of 1955. But that unique look, that Thunderbird look, the zest, the flair, and gaiety all remain the same.

But someone at Ford—it had to be a business person and not a car person—decided that the Thunder-

101

Specifications

Overall Length	205.5″	
Width	76″	
Height	54.5″/convertible	53.5″/coupe
Weight	4,600 lbs	4,400 lbs
Wheelbase	113″	
Engine	OHV V-8 390 cid/6.4 liter	
	OHV V-8 427 cid/7.0 liter	
	(optional)	
Carburetor	4 bbls 390 V-8	
	2–4 bbls 427 V-8	
Horsepower	300 @ 4,600 rpm 390 V-8	
	425 @ 6,000 rpm 427 V-8	
Bore & Stroke	4.0468″ x 3.78″ 390 V-8	
	4.23″ x 3.78 ″ 427 V-8	
Compression Ratio	10.00:1 390 V-8	
	11.50:1 427 V-8	
Electrical	12 volt	
Fuel Tank	22 gals	
Cooling System	20 qts	
Tires	8.15 x 15	
Suspension	front: ind, coil springs	
	rear: solid axle, leaf springs	
Frame	unit body	
Transmission	automatic	
Rear Axle Ratio	3.00:1	
Price	$4,900 convertible	
	$4,500 hardtop	
	$4,600 Landau	
Owner	Dick Hitt/NJ	

(The convertible shown has after market wire wheels, tire size 8.00 x 14.)

Accessories

Power Steering
Self-Adjusting Power Brakes
Power Windows
Air-Conditioning
AM/FM Radio with Rear Speaker
Leather Seats
Power Seat
Reclining Passsenger Seat
Electric Clock
Cruise Control
Power Door Locks
Remote Trunk Release
Seat Belts
Remote-Controlled Mirror, Driver's Side
Power Antenna
Tinted Class
Tonneau Cover (Changes 4-Seater into Look of 2-Seater)
4-Speed Manual Floor Shift with V-8
Heater/Defroster
Power Door Locks
Swing-Away Steering Wheel for Entering or Exiting Car
Landau Roof

bird did need some changes. The Landau roof was offered as an option. This was a padded vinyl top that eliminated the rear quarter window. It gave the car a formal or town car look—not exactly in the spirit of gaiety. The Thunderbird was selling about 6,000 convertibles a year. This obviously didn't please some other people at Ford. After 1966 there would be no more Thunderbird convertible. In 1967 Thunderbird introduced a four-door model. This would be made until 1971. A four-door Thunderbird? Landau roof, no convertible, a four-door—the people who gave you the candy were now taking it back. The spirit was gone.

1967 *Mustang*

Pony: fun, sporty, muscle, power, reasonable price, easy to service, well built, looks better today than when it was first introduced. The car was the 1967 Mustang. In two-door hardtop form with its 200 cid/6-cyl, the Mustang was pure fun and economical to maintain. Add a 289/V-8 in a convertible body, and hey, we are talking "every night is Saturday night." Add a sleek fastback design with a 390/V-8 in red, and you know this car has muscle and power written all over it.

With a base price starting at $2,500 for the two-door hardtop, the Mustang filled a gap that was left when the Thunderbird went from a two-seater to a four-seater in 1958, and upscale in price.

In its basic original form or shape the Mustang from 1964 until 1973—the last year of the real Mustang look—2,989,822 Mustangs were sold. At times it seems the Mustang is a living pony; there appear to be more on the road now than when they were new. As for "newness," the car looks as fresh today as when it first made its debut in 1964½, to be exact.

In 1968 the new 302/V-8 was added to the engine line, along with the 427/V-8 and 428/V-8, Cobra Jet. The year 1969 saw the debut of the 351/V-8 "Cleveland" engine.

For 1971 the Mustang got a slight face-lift and the convertible was now a true fun car. It had a glass rear window that was one-piece and went down with the top automatically. If you wanted, you could zip the window out for ventilation with the top up.

In 1974, the Mustang was completely revamped, and the fun, sporty, muscle-power, easy-to-service car was no more. The car may have had the name tagged on it, but to anyone who has ever owned a vintage 1964–1973 pony, there was only one true Mustang.

More Great American Dream Machines

Specifications

Overall Length	183.6"
Width	70.9"
Height	51.6"
Weight	2,900 lbs (with 390 V-8)
Wheelbase	108"
Engine	OHV straight 6-cyl 200 cid/3.3 liter
	OHV V-8 289 cid/4.7 liter
	OHV V-8 390 cid/6.4 liter
	(optional)
Carburetor	1 bbl 6-cyl
	2 bbls 289 V-8
	4 bbls 289 V-8 (optional)
	4 bbls 390 V-8 (optional)

		Compression Ratio
Horsepower	120 @ 4,400 rpm 6-cyl	9.2:1
	200 @ 4,000 rpm 2 bbls 289 V-8	9.3:1
	225 @ 4,800 rpm 4 bbls 289 V-8	
	(optional)	10.0:1
	271 @ 6,000 rpm 4 bbls 289 V-8	
	(optional)	10.5:1
	315 @ 4,600 rpm 4 bbls 390 V-8	
	(optional)	10.5:1
Bore & Stroke	3.68" x 3.12" 6-cyl	
	4.00" x 2.87" 289 V-8	
	4.05" x 3.78" 390 V-8	
Electrical	12 volt	
Fuel Tank	16 gals	
Cooling System	20½ qts/390 V-8 15 qts/289 V-8	
	9½qts/6-cyl	
Tires	6.95 x 14	
Suspension	front: ind, coil springs	
	rear: solid axle, leaf springs	
Frame	unit body	
Transmission	3-speed manual	
	3-speed heavy duty (optional on	
	390 V-8)	
	4-speed (optional)	
	automatic (optional)	
Rear Axle Ratio	3.20:1 manual	
	2.83:1 automatic	
Price	$3,100	
Owner	Roger Rohde/NJ	

Accessories

Power Steering
Power Brakes (Disc Front Only, Power Type)
Heater/Defroster
Remote-Controlled Mirror, Driver's Side
Air-Conditioning
Vinyl Roof on Hardtop
Tachometer
Seat Belts
Wire Wheel Covers
Tinted Glass
Power Convertible Top
AM Radio
AM/FM Radio
AM/FM Radio with Stereo Tape Deck
Rear Luggage Rack (Not Available on Fastback)
GT Equipment Group (Dual Exhaust, Fog Lamps,
High-Performance V-8, Disc Brakes, Racing Stripes)
Center Console
Accent Stripe
Full-Width Bench-Type Front Seat (Not Available on
Fastback)
Rally Pac Group Tach, Electric Clock, Fuel, Oil,
Temperature, and Amps Gauges
GT Equipment Group
   Dual Exhaust
   Power Front Disc Brakes
   Heavy-Duty Suspension
   Six-Inch Rims with F70 x 14 Wide Oval Tires
   Fog Lights in Grille
   GT Racing Stripe and Insignia
   GT Pop-Open–Type Gas Cap
   Painted GT Wheels with Chrome Rims
   Chrome Engine Components on 390 and 427 V-8's

1967 Shelby GT 500 (foreground); 1967 Mustang

1967 *Shelby* GT 500

The factory price was $4,195. The two center headlights were an option, which most people opted for —it was the look.

The deck lid and hood were fiberglass. The lock pins on the hood were standard, as were the air scoops. There were also air scoops (or intakes) located ahead of the rear wheels and on the roof quarter panels. On the Mustang fastback (which the GT 500 is based on) the air scoops were louvered. The rear taillights on the GT 500 are rectangular, very long and slim.

But the engine is the whole idea behind this car. That engine is a 428 cid V-8 that Ford rated conservatively at 355 hp. A more accurate rating would be somewhere around 550 hp. This is what most people in the field of performance cars agree on: The car is awesome. The car does the quarter mile in 13.5 seconds/106 mph, has a top

Specifications

Overall Length	186.6″
Width	70.9″
Height	51.6″
Weight	3,290 lbs (curb weight)
Wheelbase	108″
Engine	OHV V-8 428 cid/7.0 liter
	OHV V-8 289 cid/4.7 liter GT 350
Carburetor	4 bbls GT 500
	2–4 bbls GT 500 (optional)
	4 bbls GT 350
Horsepower	355 @ 5,400 rpm 428 V-8
	306 @ 6,000 rpm 289 V-8
Bore & Stroke	4.13″ x 3.89″ 428 V-8
	4.00″ x 2.87″ 289 V-8
Compression	10.5:1
Electrical	12 volt
Fuel Tank	16 gals
Cooling System	20½ qts
Tires	E70 x 15 low profile
Wheels	stamped steel
Rim Size	6.5″ x 15″
Suspension	front: ind, coil springs
	rear: solid axle, leaf springs
Frame	unit body
Transmission	4-speed manual all-synchronized
	(31-spline main drive)
	1st 2.32:1
	2nd 1.69:1
	3rd 1.29:1
	4th 1.00:1
	reverse 2.32:1
	Cruise-O-Matic sport shift/
	automatic (optional)
Price	$4,200
Owner	Roger Rohde/NJ

Accessories

Power Steering
Power-Front Disc Brakes
Heater/Defroster
AM Radio
AM/FM Radio
AM/FM Radio with Stereo Tape Deck
Air-Conditioning (Not Available on 428/V-8)
Tinted Windshield and Side Glass
Accent Stripe
Deluxe Steering Wheel

Remote-Control Door Mirror, Driver's Side
Folding Rear Seat
Seat Belts
Tachometer
Fuel, Oil, Amps, and Temperature Gauges
Dual Exhaust

speed of 150 mph, and yet purrs like a kitten at a traffic light.

Shelby—the name comes from Carroll Shelby, a Texan and a race car driver. In 1959 Carroll won at LeMans for Aston Martin. From 1962 until 1965 Shelby was slipping Ford V-8's into British-made A.C. Ace bodies. These cars were known as A.C. Cobras. This car coined the word "awesome"! The 1965 version with its 427 cid V-8 could go from 0 to 100 and back in 10 seconds! Just a simple 427/V-8 with 2–4 bbls Holley carburetors.

When Ford found out what Shelby was doing they asked him to help Ford with a performance car. The result was the Shelby Mustang built from 1965 until 1970. In 1968 to 1970 the car was also available as a convertible, with a roll bar.

The Shelby Mustang was everything in a car the A.C. Cobra was not. The GT 500 had roll-up side windows, power steering, a decent heater/defroster, AM/FM stereo radio with tape deck—creature comforts. The A.C. was available only as a roadster, which meant no side windows, plastic curtains were used instead, there were no locking doors, a very small trunk, and wind in your face. A great image car, but not too practical and not what most people really desire in a car.

Ford wanted a vehicle that had more comfort—heat, dryness, no rain in the face, etc. Carroll Shelby beefed up the Mustang suspension, put fifteen-inch-high performance tires on the car, redefined the fastback design, used some pearlescent paint—and gave Ford the GT 500.

1968 *Chevelle* SS 396

Just as Pontiac had their GTO and Oldsmobile their 442, Chevrolet had its little muscle car. The success of the GTO caught Chevrolet off guard.

In mid-1965 Chevrolet dropped a 396 V-8 under the hood of a Chevelle—instant muscle. Until that moment when that mighty 396 V-8 was added, the SS designation signified only special trim on the Chevelle.

The SS or Super Sport package had originally meant special deck emblems, blacked-out grille, bucket seats, center console with floor-mounted automatic, or four-speed. The engine was either the 283 V-8 or the 194 cid 6-cyl. (Imagine a Chevelle with SS trim and a 6-cyl

Specifications

Overall Length	196.8"
Width	76"
Height	52.6"
Weight	3,475 lbs
Wheelbase	112"
Engine	OHV V-8 396/6.5 liter
Carburetor	4 bbls
Horsepower	325 @ 4,800 rpm
Bore & Stroke	4.09" x 3.76"
Compression Ratio	10.25:1
Electrical	12 volt
Fuel Tank	20 gals
Cooling System	23 qts
Tires	G78 x 14
Suspension	front: ind, coil springs
	rear: solid axle, coil springs
Frame	unit body
Transmission	3-speed manual
	4-speed manual (optional)
	Turbo Hydra-Matic (optional)
Rear Axle Ratio	3.73:1
Price	$2,900
Owner	Roger Rohde/NJ

Accessories

Power Steering
Power Brakes
Power Windows
Air-Conditioning
AM/FM Stereo
AM/FM Stereo with Tape Deck
Power Disc Brakes
Heater/Defroster
Electric Clock
Center Console
Cruise Control (Not Available on Manual Shift)
Tilt Wheel
Dual Exhaust
Power Door Locks
Bucket Seats
Rear Windshield Defroster
Vinyl Roof
Rally Wheels
Amps, Fuel, Oil, and Temperature Gauges
Tachometer

under the hood?) After 1965 the SS emblem had some guts underneath it.

The SS 396 was developed with the same philosophy as the GTO. Here was a car that a young guy could afford. It was inexpensive to maintain, fun to drive, and potent when you wanted it to be. In 1968 the Chevelle was restyled with the semifastback look of the day. There was still a trunk with room and a real rear seat, but the car had a racier look than its predecessors.

The cars were real attention getters, especially among some highway patrol officers. Many of those young drivers soon learned that even at fifty mph, this car could draw attention. Those highway patrol officers stayed right on your tail to make sure you kept at fifty or sixty mph.

It took Chevrolet a little longer to respond to the Mustang. In 1967 the Camaro was unveiled.

109

1970 *Plymouth Superbird*

Y ou are not looking at some custom-type car or hot rod made in someone's garage. This exotic bird was made by Plymouth just at the tail end of the performance/muscle-car period.

What your eyes are seeing is a full-blown race car with a race car body, straight from the factory at about $3,600!

The car was a Plymouth Road Runner with a spoiler/wing to end all wings. There were two allen head bolts on either end of the wing uprights so you could adjust the pitch of the wing, depending on wind conditions and the speed you planned on going. The front end was designed for slicing through the wind at speeds of 110 mph and up The same for the roof line. That front is all metal,

Specifications

Overall Length	221″
Width	76″
Height	54″
Weight	3,789 lbs
Wheelbase	116″
Engine	OHV V-8 440 cid/7.2 liter
Carburetor	3–2 bbls (6-pack)
Horsepower	390 @ 4,700 rpm
Torque	490 @ 3,200 rpm
Bore & Stroke	4.33″ x 3.75″
Compression Ratio	10.50:1
Electrical	12 volt
Fuel Tank	19 gals
Cooling System	18.6 qts
Tires	F60 x 15
Suspension	front: ind., coil springs
	rear: solid axle, leaf springs
Frame	unit body
Transmission	Torque-Flite (3-speed automatic)
Rear Axle Ratio	3.55:1
Price	$3,600
Owner	Richard Dangler/NY

(0–60 mph in 5.9 seconds;
quarter mile in 14.2 seconds/100 mph;
top speed/140+ mph)

Accessories

Power Steering
Power Brakes
Heater/Defroster
Outside Mirror on Passenger and Driver's Side
AM Radio
Tachometer
Fuel, Oil, Amps, and Temperature Gauges
Electric Clock

not fiberglass and 17 inches long. The standard Road Runner was built on the Plymouth Belvedere chassis of 116 inches and was 204 inches long. The Superbird is 221 inches, of which 17 inches is that bolted-on front end.

The Superbird came in colors to match its looks: hemi-orange, purple, a bright slime green, and the yellow you see here.

The interior of the car was austere. This was a nuts-and-bolts dragster, not intended to be fancy on the inside. With that big performance engine, the only transmission available was the automatic three-speed Torque-Flite. Air-conditioning, cruise control, and lots of other options were not available.

To further emphasize what this car was intended for, in case you haven't noticed yet, the car has no bumper! Short runs to the supermarket were not for this Bird.

As for actual riding, to say the Superbird is firm would be polite. The seats are not the cushiony type of a Chrysler 300 of a dozen years before. The exhaust noise is deep and throaty and when all six bbls (remember this is a six-pack and that does not mean beer) kick in, the blood does seem to run a little faster.

The car does not handle the curves well, but again, for all practical purposes, this is a dragster. With that top-heavy front end, you will not take any Alpine curves at full throttle.

While this is a performance car that is quite enjoyable, the looks the car receives when just cruising are unbelievable. This is the type of car I'd go to the ballet or opera in.

The Superbird reminds you of just how wild muscle cars and the muscle car era was. It represents a mind (or no mind) and imagination gone wild, the fun end of muscle cars. See the Superbird on the upright of the wing —he's smiling!

Custom Cars, Custom Language

A spectacular part of the 50s and early 60s car scene was the "custom car" or "street rod." Oftentimes these specially designed cars were thrown into the category of "hot rods," which they are not. The term "custom" does not refer to something that rolled off a Detroit assembly line, but rather to an individual's particular vision of a particular automobile. Although any car could do, most of the cars which inevitably wound up being customized were 1949 to 1951 Mercurys and Fords.

A street rod refers to a car made prior to 1949 that has been customized. In almost every instance a street rod will have a modern engine (modern being anything from 1958 and newer) and power conveniences such as air-conditioning, power windows, etc. The cars are usually lowered anywhere from five to nine inches and given some outlandish color. The main difference between a street rod and custom car is the age of the vehicle. From 1949 and up, it is a "leadsled" custom.* From 1948 and down, "street rod" is the term.

In the early 50s there was (and still is) a midwest slang word, kemp, that means "cool" (or "kool"). Kustom Kemp as in Kustom Kemps of America are leadsleds. Before all these terms came into being, when the first Neanderthal started to modify his 1934 Ford, the term that was used for custom work was "fix-up."

A street rod can have extensive lead work performed on it, but the term leadsled (we are talking in a "purist" sense) refers to 1949 and newer. Even though any car can be used for a street rod, Fords, particularly from 1932 to 1935 and Mercurys from 1939 to 1941 are very popular (1939 was the first year for Mercury).

If owners of dream machines aren't "running on

*Leadsled: from the lead used to fill in holes and for shaping the body for a smooth look.

all eight cylinders," then the owners and designers/builders of custom/leadsled/street rods have a cracked block. Here is some more custom language:

CHOPPED: Involves the top part of the car—the glass, roof, and sitting area (or greenhouse, as it is sometimes called). Depending on the car and the individual designing the car, varying amounts of inches are "chopped" off to lower the roof. This chopping of the roof means that all glass has to be cut to fit properly in the redesigned roof. With some cars of the mid and late 50s that had curved windshields, you may be wondering how you cut curved glass . . . VERY CAREFULLY. (One small bit of information: We are talking safety-plate glass, not safety-tempered glass. Tempered glass cannot be cut. It is made to size.)

LOWERED: Lowering the suspension of the car. Again there is no set amount. If a car is lowered to within two inches of the ground, usually (but not always) either air shocks or hydraulic suspensions are added to raise the car for street driving.

CHANNELED: Cutting out the floor of the car and raising it, thus enabling the car to be lowered even more. Extreme lowering almost guarantees channeling.

SECTIONING: Major surgery that entails the slicing out of several inches in the car's midsection, all the way around for an overall lower look; the fenders, doors, firewall, and sometimes even the dashboard are sectioned and then welded back together. This procedure entails the gutting of the car. The motor and interior are removed. Sectioning is akin to a double bypass with brain surgery at the same time.

LOUVERED: Cutting louvers into the hood just for an effect. This procedure also enables heat to escape from the engine. It also allows rainwater in if there isn't some mechanism under the louvers that can be closed when it rains. (Most owners would do their best to avoid having their cars out in the rain.)

FRENCHED: A rounded, seamless effect of the fender over the headlights. It involves removing the chrome rims of the headlights, filling in the seams and holes with lead, smoothing it out and then repainting.

SHAVED: Removal of the door handles, filling in the holes and then sanding and repainting. Similar to Frenching.

NOSED AND DECKED: This does not refer to a boxing match. It does mean the removal of all chrome and emblems from the hood and trunk or deck lid, the leading-in of all holes and seams, sanding and repainting.

ROUNDED HOOD CORNERS: Just what the term implies: The cutting away of metal from the hood or fenders, and then welding and reshaping for a rounder look.

FLAMETHROWER: A specially rigged exhaust that can literally shoot flames about three to six feet. Very effective at night. At some car shows there are flame-throwing contests, to determine whose car can throw the longest flame. Also useful for melting any Japanese tin that is behind you. In the words of a female companion when she first saw this, *"WILD!"*

After all the lead is made smooth by fine sanding, just add an exotic color and you have a custom car, street rod or leadsled.

Gas-pump stereo in home of Richard Afflito/NJ

1934 *Ford Five-Window Coupe* ("*The Purple Monster*")

The second most popular car in 1934 (after Chevy) was reborn again in the 50s, and today is one of the most popular cars with hot-rodders/custom people.

In the 1950s a cult was emerging among young people that eventually became known as the NSRA, or National Street Rod Association. What these creative peo-

Specifications/Stock

Overall Length	182½"
Width	68"
Height	66"
Weight	2,643 lbs
Wheelbase	112"
Engine	L-head V-8 221 cid/3.6 liter
Carburetor	2 bbls
Horsepower	85 @ 3,800 rpm
Bore & Stroke	3.06 x 3.75
Compression Ratio	6.30:1
Electrical	6 volt
Fuel Tank	10 gals
Cooling System	22 qts
Tires	6.00 x 16
Suspension	front: I-beam, transverse leaf spring
	rear: solid axle, transverse leaf spring
Frame	all steel, body bolted on, X-member
Transmission	3-speed manual floor shift 2nd and 3rd gears synchronized
Rear Axle Ratio	4.11:1
Price	$585 (1934)
Owner	Agnes & David Romlein/NJ

Accessories/1934

Twin Horns
Wire Wheels
Parking Lights
Greyhound Hood Ornament
Twin Taillights
Fuel, Oil, Amps, and Temperature Gauges
Whitewall Tires
Dual Wipers
Banjo Wheel
Heater

ple did was to take a car from the 1930s, which most times was a Ford "deuce" (1932) coupe, and "fix it up." While new cars were going for $2,000 and up, you could pick up a 1934 Ford for $50. To give the car something extra a modern engine was put in, which was usually a Chevy V-8 that one would get at the local junkyard from a wreck. Maybe after a year or two, if the car still ran fine, a decent paint job was applied over the prime coat that the car usually sported. "Prime is fine" became an anthem for rodders of the 50s. This paint was almost always an outlandish color, a knock-'em-dead-with-laughter paint.

There were also people who saw in a 1934 Ford or 1935 Chevy a budding beauty that was ready to blossom but did not know how to do so. These people helped the car along. There are some people who think the result you see here comes from inhaling too many exhaust fumes, but to date there is no scientific data to back up that claim.

The original 1934 Ford had a 221-inch cid V-8. The rumble seat was an option. It was either a trunk for storage or had a rumble seat, which some people I spoke with (who owned these cars when they were new) referred to as "mother-in-law seats."

The 1934 Ford you see here has undergone some changes: For starters, the color is Kandy-Apple Purple over Silver by House of Kolor. The top has been chopped three inches and the front end lowered four inches. The original height of sixty-six inches is now down to an almost modern fifty-nine inches, which still affords plenty of headroom inside the car. The engine is a 305 cid Camaro V-8 matched to a 350 Turbo-Hydra-Matic transmission. The air-conditioning is supplied by Vintage Air, which is a nice unit that fits in just right with the interior aesthetics. The original 6.00 x 16 tires have been replaced by 7 x 14 wheels on the front and 7 x 15 wheels on the rear.

Modifications

Automatic Transmission Turbo-Hydra-Matic 350
Heater/Defroster
Cornering Lights
Outside Mirror Passenger and Driver's Side
Power Windows
Air-Conditioning
Overhead AM/FM Cassette Radio by Sony
Tilt Wheel
Fuel, Oil, Amps, and Temperature Gauges
1983 Chevy 305 cid/V-8 (Camaro Z-28) Engine
Rear End 9" Ford with 3.75:1 Ratio
Wheels Front: 14 x 7   Rear: 15 x 7
Brakes Front: 1972 Camaro Disc
          Rear: 1957 Ford Drum
Walker "Cool Mate" Radiator
Four-Bar Front and Rear Suspension by TCI
TCI Coil Over Shocks
Super Bell Front Axle with 4" Drop
1934 Ford Boxed Frame
All-Steel Body with 3" Chop
Silver Grey Crushed Velour Interior
Kandy Apple Purple Over Silver Paint by House of Kolor
Electrical 12 Volt
Holly 4 bbls Carburetor

On some of the original Ford coupes with rumble seats, the rear window would crank down for better ventilation and/or to enable you to talk to the person in the rumble seat—if that was possible. The front windshield would pop out from the bottom and on a warm day there would be a good flow of air through the car, an early flow-through ventilation system.

Inspirational is what this 1934 Ford is. The skin starts to tingle, the heart beats a little faster, brilliant sunsets flash across the mind. From ten-year-olds in the fifth grade to ten-year-olds sitting at an editor's desk, one single phrase comes forth from a drooling mouth: "I want that car! I want that car!"

1949 *Mercury Custom/Red*
1949 *Mercury Custom/Black*

For model year 1949 Mercury unveiled its new post-World War II look. They did not know it at the time but a cult was created that has lasted and grown to this day. The 1949 style was carried over to 1950 and 1951. In 1951 the rear lights were vertical instead of horizontal and the car was a little more square than round—just a hint of the 1952 to 1954 Mercurys that were to follow.

Whatever the reason, with a certain group of young guys across the United States, the Merc was the car to have. Some of these guys felt that as great as the Merc looked, it needed something more—or something less.

Some people took off the hood and trunk emblems, filled in the holes with lead, and then repainted so there were no telltale marks. Then maybe just lower the car a little and add more attractive fender skirts, say, from a 1951 Mercury. Then add some blue dot taillights and dual carbs, such as Offenhausers (Offys) available at the local auto parts store, some glass pack mufflers for a deep throaty sound, and this car was really starting to look good.

Of course you could go further and put in a new interior in a candy-stripe pattern, french the headlights, remove the outer rims, fill in all the holes and achieve a smooth, rounded, seamless piece of painted metal, and then shave the door handles, remove them and fill in the holes, lower the back four inches, the front two inches, get some 1956 Olds spinner hubcaps, and paint the car Candy Red. For a final touch add dual exhausts with straight pipes.

Along with this small cult of Merc-a-maniacs, there was a movie that was aimed at the youth of the country with some young, then-unknown, actors and ac-

1949 Mercury Custom/Black
Specifications/Stock

Overall Length	206.6"
Width	73"
Height	63"
Weight	3,360 lbs
Wheelbase	118"
Engine	L-head V-8 255.4 cid/4.2 liter
Carburetor	2 bbls
Horsepower	110 @ 3,600 rpm
Bore & Stroke	3.19" x 4.00"
Compression Ratio	6.80:1
Electrical	6 volt
Fuel Tank	19 gals
Cooling System	22 qts
Tires	7.10 x 15
Suspension	front: ind, coil springs, king pins
	rear: solid axle, leaf springs
Frame	X-type double drop steel
Transmission	3-speed manual
	overdrive (optional)
Rear Axle Ratio	4.27:1
Price	$2,000 (1949)
Owner	Andy Herman/NY

Accessories/Stock

Radio
Heater/Defroster
Power Windows (Standard on Convertible)
Padded Canvas or Vinyl Roof (Standard on Monterey Coupe)
Spotlight
Leather Interior
Whitewall Tires
Power Seat

Modifications

Nosed and Decked
Deck with Electric Solenoid
2" Lower in Rear
1951 Mercury Skirts
Dual Exhaust straight pipes with no mufflers
Blue Dot Taillights
Dual Carbs and Headers

tresses. Some of their names were Sal Mineo, Natalie Wood, and a newcomer—James Dean. The movie was *Rebel Without a Cause*. In it James Dean drove a 1950 Mercury. There was no turning back this car now.

To a few automobile "purists," it is blasphemy to tamper with a car's design or original mechanics. But this is the United States and one of the freedoms guaranteed in the Constitution is the freedom to customize '50s Mercurys.

The two 1949 Mercurys seen here and owned by Andy Herman are typical examples of mild customizing. They have not been chopped or channeled as in the case of a radical sled. They are prime examples of what many 1949 to 1951 Mercurys looked like in the mid-50s. Except some were often left with a prime coating. ("Prime is fine.")

The people who own, design, and build these custom chariots of the gods are in many ways the embodiment of the American dream and the pioneer spirit. They dare to be different and are going off into the wilderness, so to speak, on a mission that will not be known until finally completed. Some of the designers and builders of these cars are literally legends in their own time: Barris, Proffit, Metz, Winfield, and Dunn. One hundred years from now many of these cars will probably be appreciated as true art forms.

Today you can enjoy these cars for what they are: mobile sculptures on wheels. It's true that most custom/leadsled owners have a little too much oil in their veins and some brain tissue damage from all those fumes; but they are people too and their work should be respected. Remember: They laughed at Columbus and the Wright Brothers, and Michelangelo only did walls and ceilings; he never did the hard part, the outside.

To repeat: If the car was made prior to 1949 it is

a street rod. From 1949 on it is a leadsled or custom. When the NSRA has its annual spring and summer meets or shows held in various locations from Lexington, KY, to York, PA, and St. Paul, MN, about 10,000 to 11,000 rods show up. That is a Rose Bowl parking lot with just cars that are no newer than 1948. When the Custom Kemps of America hold their annual spring and summer shows, only about 4,000 to 5,000 sleds from 1949 and up can be seen.

Just remember that if you attend any of these

1949 Mercury Custom/Red
Specifications/Stock

Overall Length	206.6"
Width	73"
Height	63"
Weight	3,369 lbs
Wheelbase	118"
Engine	L-Head V-8 255.4 cid/4.2 liter
Carburetor	2 bbls
Horsepower	110 @ 3,600 rpm
Bore & Stroke	3.19" x 4.00"
Compression Ratio	6.80:1
Electrical	6 volt
Fuel Tank	19 gals
Cooling System	22 qts
Tires	7.10 x 15
Suspension	front: ind, coil springs, king pins rear: solid axle, leaf springs
Frame	X-type double drop steel
Transmission	3-speed manual overdrive (optional)
Rear Axle Ratio	4.27:1
Price	$2,000 (1949)
Owner	Andy Herman/NY

Accessories

AM Radio
Heater/Defroster
Power Windows (Standard on Convertible)
Leather Interior
Padded Canvas or Vinyl Top (Standard on Monterey Coupe)

Modifications

Candy Stripe Rolled and Pleated Interior
Frenched Headlights
Bull-Nosed Front
Rounded Hood Corners
Molded Grille Shell
Custom Grille Center
Spotlights
Shaved Doors with Electric Solenoids
4" Lowering Blocks/Rear
2" Lowering Blocks/Front
Shaved Trunk with Electric Solenoid
Blue Dot Taillights
1956 Oldsmobile Spinner Hubcaps
1951 Mercury Skirts
Original Engine with: After-Market Dual Carbs and
                      Headers
                      Mallory Ignition
                      Aluminum High-Compression
                      Heads
Dual Exhaust with Glass Packs
BEAUTIFUL

shows as a first-time looker, be careful. Many of the people who own these cars from all outward appearances seem to be normal. They are anything but! You may even be enticed to come to another show, which could lead to a barbecue with some real beef or shrimp, cold beer, and no bottled water. It may even lead to what these people refer to as camaraderie. So take heed, you were forewarned.

1951 Mercury Custom/ Candy Berry Wine

T he 1951 Mercury seen here in the fantastic color candy berry wine is living proof of what inhaling the fumes of leaded gas can do to the mind—in this particular instance, the mind of "Wildman" Bob Ferenczi.

Specifications

Overall Length	206.8"
Width*	73"
Height*	63"
Weight	3,700 lbs
Wheelbase	118"
Engine	OHV V-8 350 cid Oldsmobile/ 5.7 liter
Carburetor	650 Holley 4 bbls
Horsepower	350 @ 4,800 rpm
Bore & Stroke	4.057" x 3.385"
Compression Ratio	10.25:1
Electrical	12 volt
Fuel Tank	19 gals
Cooling System	16½ qts
Tires	7.10 x 15
Suspension	front: late-model 1982 Oldsmobile subframe grafted to original Mercury rear: solid axle, leaf springs (original Mercury)
Frame	X-type with 1982 Olds subframe
Transmission	1986 Corvette 4-speed automatic overdrive
Rear Axle Ratio	3.30:1
Price	$2,150 (1951)
Owner	Bob Ferenczi/NY

*The width and height are stock 1951 Mercury. This car has been lowered approximately 9" and lengthened 2½".

The effects of fooling around with cars and engines most of his life and inhaling exhaust resulted in delusions of the mind and hallucinatory visions of some grand car of which this Merc is the final product.

Bob, with the help of some friends, designed and built this fabulous automobile, from the taking apart and welding in of the new subframe, to the installation of the new motor, to the chopping of the top and the final step of painting the car candy berry wine. Just those words inspire the mind to visions of endless Saturday nights.

Modifications

Nosed & Decked
1954 Mercury Taillights and Headlight Rims
Four Air Shocks (Front and Rear), with Two Cadillac
Compressors Which Can Lift Car 4"
1947 Oldsmobile Grille, 1949 Mercury Cavity
1958 Oldsmobile Steering Wheel Mounted on Pontiac
Tilt Column
Smitty's Steel Pack Mufflers
Tinted Glass
Rear Fenders Extended 4" to Accommodate 1954
Mercury Taillights
Chassis has been cut (Channeled) and Reconstructed
to Accommodate Low Ride. Rear of Car Has Been
Lowered 4"
Power Steering
AM/FM Tape Deck
6-Way Power Seat/Leather 1982 Cadillac
Air-Conditioning
Power Brakes
Remote Trunk Release
Fuel, Oil, Amps, and Temperature Gauges
Electric Clock
Heater/Defroster
Power Antenna

As for the car, Bob has extended the rear four inches to accommodate the 1954 Mercury taillights. The roof has been chopped four inches in front and six inches in the rear, with the same being done to the front and rear glass and side windows as well. The chassis has been cut out and reconstructed (channeled) to accommodate the low ride.

The headlight rims are also from a 1954 Mercury. The grill is a stock 1947 Oldsmobile grille in a 1949 Mercury cavity with Smitty's steel pack mufflers for a rich throaty sound. The steering wheel is from a 1958 Olds mounted on a Pontiac tilt column. The air-conditioning, power windows, AM/FM tape deck, and power seat are 1982 Cadillac.

There are air shocks front and rear with two Cadillac compressors enabling the car to be lifted up four inches when necessary, depending on the surface and condition of the road.

The final result is a leadsled/cruiser just waiting for the submarine races to start. This is the type of car that on a warm summer night pulls up slowly in front of some house framed with a forsythia hedge: The sun is just starting to sink, the sky is aglow in bright shades of orange and red, and the girl's mother emerges from the backyard pool, takes one look at this car, and says, "No way is my daughter going out with the guy who drives this car . . . I AM!"

1951 Mercury Custom/ Dark Teal and White

Unlike some radical leadsleds or customs, this 1951 Mercury is a mild custom. It has not had its roof chopped, its chassis lowered, or its floor channeled. The only lead work in this car was done on its rear fenders to accommodate the 1954 Mercury taillights and the nosed and decked hood and trunk lid. It also has a 396 V-8 under the hood.

126

Specifications

Overall Length*	206.6"
Width*	73"
Height*	63"
Weight	3,485 lbs
Wheelbase	118"
Engine	OHV V-8 396 cid Chevrolet/ 6.5 liter
Carburetor	Holley 4 bbls
Horsepower	325 @ 4,800 rpm
Bore & Stroke	4.094" x 3.76"
Compression Ratio	10.25:1
Electrical	12 volt
Fuel Tank	19 gals
Cooling System	oversized radiator/23 qts
Tires	7.10 x 15 (1951) G78 x 15 (today)
Suspension	front: 1969 Chevrolet Nova subframe rear: 1963 Ford, 9" leaf springs
Frame	Chevrolet subframe welded to 1951 Mercury
Transmission	1985 Corvette 700R overdrive
Rear Axle Ratio	3.72:1 Ford 9"
Price	$2,150 (1951)
Owner	John Modafferi/NY

Modifications

1954 Mercury Frenched Headlight Rims
1954 Chevrolet Grille with Extra Teeth
1953 Buick Side Trim
1947 Lincoln Door Buttons
1954 Mercury Taillights
Rear Fenders Extended 3"
Nosed and Decked
Lowered 5½"
Cadillac Tilt Steering Post and Original Steering Wheel
Power Steering and Brakes
Automatic Transmission with Overdrive
Heater/Defroster
Power Windows
Remote Trunk Release
AM/FM Radio
Fuel, Oil, Amps, and Temperature Gauges
Tinted Glass
Electric Clock
Air-Conditioning

John Modafferi, with the help of some very good friends, did all the work on this car in his one-car garage. You may be wondering what John does for a living. Is this his profession? If we are to use the definition of a professional as someone who earns a livelihood in their field of endeavor, then this car had no professional work performed on it. But if the definition of professional is characterized by or conforming to the technical or ethical standards of a profession, then artisans of the highest caliber performed a labor of love on this car.

The Mercurys of this era, 1949 to 1956, seem to have come from the heavens. The 1949 to 1951s in particular are almost godlike. No matter what you do to them they look great. If you leave them intact and just add a special color, the cars look spectacular. Take some chrome off and chop a little off the roof, and the car still looks great, still looks like a Mercury, and yet it is different, a personal statement by whomever owns the car.

The 1949 Mercury differed slightly from the 1950 in its rear-window treatment. The 1950 had a one-piece rear window. In 1949 the rear window had two chrome strips dividing the window into a big center with two smaller side sections.

In 1951 the Mercury's taillights were vertical and the rear slightly squared off, as opposed to the more rounded 1949–1950 look, which had horizontal taillights. The taillights from a 1954 Mercury would not work on a 1949 or 1950 Mercury.

If the 1955–1957 Thunderbirds are the "blondes" of cars, then the 1949–1951 Mercurys are the "black-haired" beauties!

*The length, width, and height are stock 1951 Mercury. This car has been lowered 5½" and lengthened 2½".

127

1953 *Mercury Custom/Red*
1953 *Mercury Custom/Heather*

The basic length, width, and height specifications for the original Mercury are given. The red car has been lowered four inches, the heather car, two inches. This was done by lowering the suspension and not cutting the top or cutting anything out of the sheet metal.

Nosed and decked refers to removal of all chrome and hood or trunk lid ornamentation, leading in the holes that are left, and then smoothing this out and painting the hood and trunk/nose and deck. It presents a smooth, un-cluttered look.

Shaved door handles is the removal of the door handles, filling in and smoothing the holes, and repaint-

1953 *Mercury Custom/Red* Specifications

Overall length*	202.2″
Width*	74″
Height*	62.2″
Weight	3,700 lbs
Wheelbase	118″
Engine	OHV V-8 cid Chevrolet/5.7 liter
Carburetor	3–2 bbls
Horsepower	360 @ 4,800 rpm
Bore & Stroke	4.00″ x 3.48″
Compression Ratio	10.25:1
Electrical	12 volt
Fuel Tank	19 gals
Cooling System	16½ qts
Tires	7.60 x 15
Suspension	front: ind., coil springs rear: solid axle coil springs
Frame	X-type
Transmission	Turbo 400 automatic
Rear Axle Ratio	3.30:1
Price	$2,250 (1953)
Owner	Richard Afflito/NJ

*The length, width, and height are stock, 1953. The car has been lowered approximately 4″

Modifications

1957 Cadillac Hubcaps
Stainless Steel Lake Pipes
Foxcraft Skirts
Lowered 4″ All Around
Nosed and Decked
Frenched Headlights
1956 Packard Taillights
Custom Continental Kit
1954 Mercury Rear Bumper
1965 Buick Skylark Interior
Custom Lift-Off Convertible Top with Diamond Window
Color: Porsche Indian Red
Full Instrumentation
Tachometer
Clarion Stereo
Power Antenna
Shaved Door Handles
Dual Exhaust
Dummy Spotlights (Not Working)
1969 Camaro Subframe & Rear
350 Chevy Engine with 3–2's

1953 Mercury Custom/Heather

Specifications

Overall Length*	202.2"
Width*	74"
Height*	62.2"
Weight	3,700 lbs
Wheelbase	118"
Engine	OHV V-8 351 Ford/5.7 liter
Carburetor	4 bbls
Horsepower	285 @ 5,400 rpm
Bore & Stroke	4.00" x 3.50"
Compression Ratio	10.7:1
Electrical	12 volt
Fuel Tank	19 gals
Cooling System	20½ qts
Tires	7.60 x 15
Suspension	front: ind., coil springs
	rear: solid axle, leaf springs
Frame	X-type
Transmission	Automatic
Rear Axle Ratio	3.50:1
Price	$2,250 (1953)
Owner	Michael Afflito/NJ

Modifications

Nosed and Decked
Frenched Headlights
Foxcraft Skirts
Lee Custom Taillights
1982 Buick Interior
1958 Oldsmobile Paint, Color: Heather
1956 Mercury Spinners
Lake Pipes
Full instrumentation Via VDO Vintage Gauges
Recessed Power Antenna
Wide Whites
1954 Mercury Side Teeth
C6 Automatic Transmission
Shaved Door Handles
Dual Exhaust
Working Spotlight
Blaupunkt Stereo
Custom Lift-Off Convertible Top

ing. Usually there is a button on the underside of the car that you press with your foot to open the door, or if the window is open, you can just reach in and open from the inside.

Custom lift-off top: These two cars were originally hardtops. The top was cut off and special, custom-made tops were put on. They do not fold, so if the top is removed the weather for the day had better be good. When on, the top looks like a convertible top.

On many customs or leadsleds spotlights do not work. The spots are for decoration purposes most of the time. In the case of the heather-colored Mercury, the owner prefers to have a working spotlight. The cost is the same for a working or nonworking one.

Lake pipes are on both cars. These are the chrome pipes on the side of each car that look like exhaust pipes (though these do not work).

In the terminology of Custom Kemps/Leadsleds, these two Mercs would fall into the mild custom category. They have not been chopped, sectioned, or channeled.

*The length, width, and height are stock, 1953. This car has been lowered approximately 2".

1956 *Mercury Montclair Custom*

In 1955 Mercury started doing to their cars at the factory what individuals had been doing to them since the late 1940s. Mercury was turning out custom-type cars because that is what the public wanted.

The Frenched (hooded) headlights came straight from the production line. Want more? Mercury was there with rear fender skirts, continental kit, two-tone paint combinations, dual exhaust, and a lavish two-tone color interior—with the roll and pleat from the factory.

But some people are never satisfied until something is truly stamped with their personal signature. The

Specifications

Overall Length	206.4″ (without continental kit)
Width	76.4″
Height	58.8″
Weight	3,500 lbs
Wheelbase	119″
Engine	OHV V-8 312 cid/5.1 liter
Carburetor	4 bbl
Horsepower	225 @ 4,600 rpm
Bore & Stroke	3.80 x 3.44
Compression Ratio	9.0:1
Electrical	12 volt
Fuel Tank	18 gals
Cooling System	20 qts
Tires	7.60 x 15
Suspension	front: ind., coil springs, ball joints rear: solid axle, leaf springs
Frame	X-type
Transmission	Merc-O-Matic
Rear Axle Ratio	3.54:1
Price	$3,300
Owner	Joe Verdi/NY

Accessories

Fuel, Amp, Oil, and Temperature Gauges
Remote Trunk Release
Continental Kit
Self-Lubrication System (At the Push of a Button the
Driver Could Lubricate the Car with Its Self-Contained
Reservoir in the Trunk—a Real Jiffy Lube.)
Power Steering
Power Brakes
Power Windows
Heater/Defroster
Air-Conditioning
Electric Clock
Radio with Rear Speaker
Power Antenna
Rear Window Defogger
Fender Skirts
Seat Belts
Color: Mint Green/Bone White

1956 Mercury seen here—"Heart Throb," and she is truly that—has had some personal touches added by its owner, Joe Verdi. Some people say Joe has inhaled too much hydraulic fluid but there is no medical evidence to substantiate that claim.

The motor is still the original 312 cid V-8 mated to the original Merc-O-Matic automatic transmission. The interior is all original, as is the paint. As for the custom part:

nosed and decked
lowered two inches
louvered hood—180 louvers
special continental kit
shaved door handles
power doors (open and close)
one-bar Flipper hubcaps
rolled and pleated trunk

If this '56 Merc doesn't get your heart or other parts of the body throbbing, pack it in; you've been plasticized.

1963 *Mercury Comet Custom Pickup*

Your eyes and mind are not deceiving you. This is a pickup and, no, Mercury never had one in the Comet lineup. George Edwards bought the Comet new. After owning the car for about twelve years, he grew tired of the car in sedan form. He liked the size and performance of the car, but he wanted something different, something he could use to throw parts in when he was out at car shows and flea markets looking for parts for his other cars (as in 1947 Continental, 1963 Continental, etc.).

George never liked the design of the Falcon Ranchero–type vehicle. He owns a 1963 Falcon coupe, but

Specifications

Overall Length	194.8″
Width	70.4″
Height	54.5″
Weight	2,400 lbs
Wheelbase	114″
Engine	OHV straight 6-cyl 170 cid/2.8 liter/ optional
	OHV straight 6-cyl 144 cid/2.3 liter
Carburetor	1 bbl
Horsepower	101 @ 4,400 rpm 170 6-cyl
	85 @ 4,200 rpm 144 6-cyl
Bore & Stroke	3.50″ x 2.94″ 170 6-cyl
	3.50″ x 2.50″ 144 6-cyl
Compression Ratio	8.70:1 170 6-cyl/144 6-cyl
Electrical	12 volt
Fuel Tank	14 gals
Cooling System	9.3 qts
Tires	6.50 x 13
Suspension	front: ind., coil springs
	rear: solid axle, leaf springs
Frame	unit body
Transmission	Merc-O-Matic (optional)
	3-speed manual
	4-speed manual (optional)
Rear Axle Ratio	3.50:1
Price	$2,250 (in 1963)
Owner	George M. Edwards/NJ

Accessories

OHV V-8 260 cid 3.5 liter Engine (Optional)
Backup Lights
Air-Conditioning
Luggage Rack on Station Wagon
Two-Tone Paint
Electric Tailgate on Station Wagon
Padded Dashboard
Heater/Defroster
Rear Window Defogger
AM Radio
Fuel and Temperature Gauges
Windshield Washer
Power Steering
Power Brakes

always thought the Comet would look better as a pickup or Ranchero type. So George did what any person who has inhaled too many exhaust fumes would do, he designed and had built his own Comet-chero. The rear window is the rear window from the sedan that was cut for this purpose. The wooden floor bed can be lifted up piece by piece for easy access to the undercarriage. The interior/front seat is from the sedan. The car has not been altered in any dimensional aspect except for the removal of the rear passenger compartment and trunk.

Then there is the color: dark green and lime green, which truly makes this car a knockout. When I first happened onto George and his Comet, we were going opposite directions on a back road. I made a U-turn and immediately took off after what I thought at the time was some rare factory car I had never seen before. I was flashing my headlights and sounding my horn. George thought I was crazy and maybe dangerous (he told me later on he was half right). Charlie, George's brother, was in the Comet and happened to mention to George that I was driving an Eldorado convertible; maybe I wanted to ask them something about the car.

At those words from Charlie, George finally pulled off to the shoulder. The rest is, as the phrase goes, history. Several weeks later, when I phoned to make arrangements to photograph the Comet, George mentioned that he and Charlie owned some other cars that I might be interested in, but I would have to be the judge of that. One of those cars is the impeccable 1947 Continental on pages 5–8.

The most important result of this episode was getting to know George and Charlie (as in the case with all of the other incredible people whose cars I have photographed). As spectacular as the Comet and Continental are, they pale next to George and Charlie.

Appendixes

Where to Find a Car

There is no one special place to find a dream machine, although I personally believe that every car ever made is waiting for a new owner in New Jersey and Pennsylvania. These two states—New Jersey in particular—have an incredible amount of old tin on the road that people are obviously enjoying.

Whatever can be said about the motor vehicle bureau of New Jersey, it is kind to old cars. It makes the registering of such cars a breeze. Someone seems to recognize the value (and not only monetary) of old cars in New Jersey and Pennsylvania.

Buy the local newspapers where you live and other local publications that serve people with merchandise to sell. These publications have names such as *Want Ads, Selling Post, Buy Lines,* etc. Find out about the publications in your area.

The publications listed under Car Publications (page 142) not only have ads for cars for sale but also list car auctions and car shows/flea markets. Go to those in your area and get a feeling of what some cars are worth in a certain condition. After a short time you will be able to note the difference in the superficial condition of one car compared to another that is really in fine condition.

If you have a good pair of boots and don't mind some dust or mud (depending on the weather), go to Hershey, PA, around the first weekend in October. You will have some company in the form of about 150,000 to 200,000 other oil-in-their-veins car nuts. In an area about a mile long and a half a mile wide, all the eye will see is car parts and cars, anything from a Buick to a Willys from model year 1903 to a new car, which at Hershey means twenty-five years old or older.

The weekend before Hershey, there is a flea market at Carlisle, PA, which is about thirty miles from Hershey. This is mostly for post–World War II cars and parts with a heavy emphasis on the 1960s and early 1970s muscle cars. Carlisle only attracts about 100,000 people looking over the wares of about 8,000 vendors spread out over 200 acres. There is also an area called the "car corral," where over 2,000 cars are for sale by individuals. See what you like, cash on the barrel head, and off you go. Or, if you are not already having a coronary from the asking price, make arrangements to purchase the car wherever it is convenient for you and the owner of the vehicle to meet afterward.

But getting back to Hershey (where many of the Carlisle vendors also go), this is the granddaddy of car shows. There are about 9,000 vendors for three days selling/buying auto parts from spark plugs for a Pierce Arrow to fenders for a '48 Olds.

The final day, which is a Saturday, is also show day. Here is where you will see over

2,500 cars. This is where a person who owns a Duesenberg three rows over passes your 1951 Rambler and says, "Nice car," and means it!

Hershey is where that "farmer" in overalls with the pickup parked in his vendor spot just happens to own five acres in Greenwich, CT, with about twenty-five cars housed on the property. The "cowboy" he is selling those parts to has a "couple of T-Birds and '59 Eldo's on the ranch," in New Jersey.

This is America—capitalism, individualism, and dream machines.

How to Find a Car

Go out and buy one. This does not mean that you should buy the first car you see or spend a fortune. But buy some old sedan with character, a car that has been cared for by an "older couple" or person. With a little elbow grease, a shine can probably be brought back to the paint. You will soon discover that the car is more dependable than you thought, easier to maintain, and less costly to repair than your newer car.

This little buggy will also make it easier for you to meet people, people with other "old cars." It is much easier to stop someone in the dream machine you covet when you are driving a 1963 Rambler Classic or 1957 Pontiac sedan. This little machine will take you to car shows, to auctions, into people's hearts until the day you see your dream machine—or it sees you.

How to Restore a Car

Restoring a car can mean anything from replacing a hubcap or getting the proper whitewall width for the tires to completely dismantling the auto down to the chassis and rebuilding or replacing everything—the motor, the pumps, the wiring, the interior—and finally repainting in a factory color for that year of car. Remember, no car ever left the factory with more than five to seven coats of paint. Anything more than seven or eight coats and in a short time you will have cracks or "a roadmap of the United States." Twenty-coat paint jobs are just hype, and if in fact a car does have twenty coats, stay away.

The actual painting of the car is fairly easy—not trying to put any painters down; it is the preparation and condition of the car before the paint is applied that is most important. All the paint does is reflect the preparation and work that went before it (if it is a properly done paint job to begin with).

Today many cars are overrestored. They look better than the day they left the factory. Some cars have engine compartments that look better than most new cars and undercarriages

136

you can eat off of. A 1957 Chevy Bel Air was built to drive, not to be hauled around on a car trailer.

Cars were meant to be driven, if only for a weekend of fun or going to a car show. With this philosophy in mind when it comes time for a repaint, if that is necessary, if there is a particular shade of blue or red that was not available for your car when new, or if you have a Ford and like a Lincoln color better, go for it. The key word here is "fun"! When the car hobby ceases to be fun or a source of enjoyment, get out. I know many people who own twenty or more cars. They could be called "investments." But to these people they are fun. They just bought the candy store instead of the candy.

As for a "restoration" shop and what it does, this type of service garage is prepared to take your car down to the chassis and rebuild the car piece by piece. It has the facilities to keep your car for an extended period of time—up to two years, in some cases. Some restoration shops even do their own interior work. Others "farm out" interior work as well as all rechroming and replating. Of course you pay for this.

You can also check around in your local community for a competent mechanic, a good body shop, and an interior shop. It is not as difficult as you may think to find these specialty shops.

Some of the best restorations I have seen have been done by individuals right in their own one-car garage. Competence isn't measured by the size or waiting area the service garage has.

How to Find Parts, Supplies, and Repair Shops

One of the most useful items in finding any of the above is your brain. If you do not or will not take the time to research what you need—get the correct part number off the part you need, know the size engine on your vehicle, what type of transmission you have, etc.—you will have a difficult and expensive time.

Many of the parts for "old cars" can be found at local auto parts stores, if you invest a little time and effort in knowing what you need. Pressure hoses can be made to order while you wait by many auto parts stores, if they have the old one to copy. Hard parts, such as power steering pumps or water pumps, can be rebuilt if not readily available. Hard in this case means solid, something that is not made of plastic such as generators, alternators, etc.

As for parts numbers, depending on the engine, on some models a master cylinder may be different for one engine as opposed to another. When calling for a part, know as much about your car as possible. The owner's manual is a good place to start. You may have to make five or six phone calls instead of one, but it is worth it.

In many instances you will find repair shops more willing and eager to work on an "old car." Many new cars offer very little challenge to a true mechanic's ability. They are more robotlike. Good mechanics like to listen to an engine, to hear it talk back. New cars are poor conversationalists.

Keep an eye out for repair shops with an old pickup, 1957 Ford or 1965 'Vette parked there—that's the place you want! If you have a new car for daily transportation, get to know the service people at the local dealership. You'd be surprised at how many service technicians at new car dealerships own a dream machine.

The following is just a small group of people who are reliable, courteous, and knowledgeable. Kind of like dream machines themselves, "they don't make 'em like that anymore." As for price, that is for you to find out. Remember, these people make a living at their particular business, and they depend on repeat business to maintain their growth. They also like old cars. Many got into business as a hobby or to find parts for themselves and "never grew up."

Use the businesses and individuals who advertise in *Hemmings*, *Cars and Parts*, and *Old Cars Weekly*. Too bad more American corporations aren't run the way many of these businesses are.

I have dealt with many of the following businesses and have had friends who have had good dealings to report also. If you get a part from any of these people, your local mechanic will be able to do the work. Dream machines are usually simpler to work on than new cars.

Parts, Supplies, and Repair Shops

KANTER AUTO PRODUCTS
76 Monroe Street
Boonton, NJ 07005
800-526-1096
201-334-9575

Fred and Dan started out supplying parts for Packards (they own several). They now have the world's largest inventory of Packard parts. In addition they also have mechanical parts for almost any American car—old car, that is. Also have paint and leather hides. Dan's everyday car is a 1955 Packard. Fred alternates between a mid-60s wagon and one of his Packards.

JOHN KEPICH (exhaust systems)
Box 15
16270 Old US 41 South
Fort Meyers, FL 33912
800-365-5764

Makes complete exhaust systems for any car. Also will make systems in stainless steel.

FATSCO TRANSMISSION PARTS
81 US Highway #46
Fairfield, NJ 07006
201-227-2487

Will rebuild your transmission or sell you the parts. They (Russ) know transmissions! Will ship anywhere.

POWER HYDROS/TRANSMISSION & POWER STEERING
3099 Cropsey Avenue
Brooklyn, NY 11224
718-266-4430

Rebuilds transmissions—the right way.

PALM BEACH MOTORS, INC.
Closter Dock Road
Alpine, NJ 07620
201-784-8408

From a tune-up to a restoration. Randy and John especially like Corvettes and fins.

BILL HIRSCH (no relation)
396 Littleton Avenue
Newark, NJ 07103
800-828-2601
201-642-2404
> Paint, convertible-top material, upholstery, and leather, wheel trim rings, Packard parts, etc.

MAX PENN & SON
219 Johnson Avenue
Brooklyn, NY 11206
718-497-1333
> Auto interiors, convertible tops. In business seventy years. What they forgot, most people do not even know.

BATTERY SPECIALIST OF NEW YORK
369-375 Park Avenue
Brooklyn, NY 11205
718-852-0555/0574

82 Allen Blvd.
East Farmingdale, NY 11735
516-752-0011
> Any type of battery. Carries large inventory of old-style black rubber batteries in six and twelve volt.

A-ONE TRANSMISSION PARTS
653 11th Avenue
New York, NY 10036
212-581-7490
> Transmission parts only. Very good.

VINTAGE PARTS HOUSE
93 Whippany Road
Morristown, NJ 07960
201-539-5307
> Mechanical parts for mostly GM cars, 1936 and up.

FICKEN AUTO PARTS
132 Calvert Avenue, Box 11
Babylon, NY 11702
516-587-3332
> Large supply of Trico wiper motors and can rebuild almost any old wiper motor. Also original distributor caps, points, etc. for cars 1931 and up.

AUTO PARTS EXCHANGE
P.O. Box 736
Reading, PA 19603
215-372-2813
> Lincoln parts 1953–1983 . . . know and love Lincolns, especially early 1960s.

STONE BARN, INC.
Rt. 46/Box 117
Vienna, NJ 07880
201-637-4444
> From a Dodge to a Deuce as in Duesenberg. For some old-world craftsmanship, just go to Vienna—Vienna, NJ. From a tune-up to a complete restoration, they do it all.

BEVERLY HILLS CAR COVERS
200 S. Robertson Blvd
Dept. HM11
Beverly Hills, CA 90211
1-800-421-0911
213-657-4664/FAX
> Car covers in all cotton and Stormguard for outdoor use.

RELIABLE CAR COVERS
1751-H12 Spruce St.
Riverside, CA 92507
1-800-854-4770
714-781-3060/FAX
> Car covers in poly/cotton blend Durashield for outdoor use.

COUNTRY AUTO BODY
Rt. 340 and Valentine Road
Sparkhill, NY 10976
914-359-4565
> From a Mercury to a Mercedes 300SL. Small shop that does things the old-fashioned way . . . with pride and care. "It's either good or no good . . . not good enough."

BROWNFELD AUTO SPRINGS INC.
319 10th Avenue
NYC, NY 10001
212-265-3088
    Springs, front end work, coil springs a specialty.

COHEN AUTO SPRINGS
2845 Atlantic Avenue
Brooklyn, NY 11207
718-277-0310
    Springs, ball joints, front end work, est. 1919.

LEOGRANDE
171 Hope St.
Brooklyn, NY 11211
718-384-7088
    Mechanical repairs and body work. Thinks FORD means "fix or repair daily."

RNA AUTOMOTIVE
1010 Oakley Park Road
Walled Lake, MI 48088
    Reproduction rubber parts.

JUST SUSPENSION
P.O. Box 167
Towaco, NJ 07082
201-335-0547
    American cars, 1937–1979. Ball joints, tie rod ends, king pins, etc.

HUBCAP STORE
Easton, PA
201-252-1421
    Wheel covers and hubcaps for almost any car.

RESTORATION SPECIALTIES and SUPPLY
P.O. Box 32S Dept A
Windber, PA 15963
814-467-9842
    Window channels, trim moldings, door and trunk weather stripping.

HIBERNIA AUTO RESTORATION
Maple Terrace
Hibernia, NJ 07842
201-627-1882
    From a flat tire to a complete restoration, from a 1951 Rambler to a 1936 Packard.

STEELE
1601 Hwy 150 East
Denver, NC 28037
800-544-8665
    Windshield rubber, suspension rubber, weather stripping, etc.

HILL & VAUGHN
1607 Lincoln Blvd.
Santa Monica, CA 90404
213-450-8684
    Mechanical and body work to a complete restoration.

THE STUDEBAKER SHOP
Altus, OK 73521
    Studebaker parts, especially for pickups.

ARTHUR GOULD
6 Delores Lane
Fort Salonga, NY 11768
516-754-5010
    Fuel pumps/water pumps.

CONVERTIBLE SERVICE
5126 H Walnut Grove Avenue
San Gabriel, CA 91776
    Convertible-top motors, cylinders, hoses. Will rebuild your old motor.

How to Insure an Old Car

"Does it cost a fortune to insure all those cars? Are all those cars insured? How do I get my car insured?" These are the three most-asked questions by people who are not in the hobby of old cars. The answers are no, yes, and read on.

Insurance brokers and sales agents usually know less about antique/special-interest car insurance than the person who is inquiring about the insurance. I was lucky with my first car (which I still have). My broker inquired about an antique type of insurance policy and then insured the car, no hassle (1976).

The following companies/brokers specialize in antique/special-interest car insurance. They know their business and are reputable. Stay away from the insurance company that advertises "low rates . . . no license, no problem, eighteen speeding tickets, we'll insure you, still get our low rate." There was a company like this in the northeast several years ago. There was only one small hitch: They took your money but never issued a policy. The company is now out of business.

The companies listed here are knowledgeable and courteous. They will answer any question you or your broker will have. (They do not charge more if you go through your own agent or broker.)

AMERICAN COLLECTORS
P.O. Box 8343
385 North Kings Highway
Cherry Hill, NJ 08034
800-257-5758
609-779-7212

CONDON & SKELLY
121 East Kings Highway/Suite 203
Maple Shade, NJ 08052
800-257-9496
800-624-4688 (in New Jersey)
609-234-3434

THE GRUNDY AGENCY
P.O. Box 68
Glenside, PA 19038
800-338-4005
215-887-8100

J.C. TAYLOR
320 South 69th St.
Upper Darby, PA 19082
800-345-8290
800-552-3535 (in Pennsylvania)
215-853-1300

How to Determine the Value of an Old Car

"Try and sell it." That is what a friend says. If there is a buyer then you know what it is worth. But how to determine that "price"? Or how do you know if you are not paying too much?

There is a publication, _Old Car Price Guide_. It is just that. It takes a composite of cars from auctions and dealers and then prints an "average" for a guide. This is just for a foundation.

Go to auctions and flea markets. Make someone an offer and see if they accept it. Go to dealers who specialize in collector cars and see what "the bottom line" is. Some dealers and auction companies say certain collector cars go up 20 percent or more a year. Ask them: If you pay $20,000 for the car you like today, will they buy it back in a year for $25,000? Unless you have money to burn, buy the car you like, your dream machine, not an "investment car." If you drive it, enjoy it and maintain it, you will never lose—and will probably make a profit when and if you ever decide to sell it.

I know an individual who purchased a Duesenberg in 1950 for $300. In 1959 the car was sold for $7,000. This person was the happiest person in the world—then. In 1980 the same car sold for $120,000, and in 1987 it went for $700,000. If I could predict the future, I wouldn't be doing this book.

The "best" cars usually change hands from individual to individual and never make it to the auction block or dealer's floor.

Buy the dream machine you like.

Car Publications

The following publications are worth looking at to broaden your knowledge of the old car hobby, not only to find parts, but to have a ballpark value of cars and to find out where and when there are shows and meets near where you live.

The two biggest meets are in Hershey and Carlisle, PA, in the fall every year. The exact dates are given in Hemmings Motor News and Old Cars Weekly.

Hemmings Motor News
Box 100
Bennington, VT 05201
If you get one publication, get this one. It is THE BIBLE.

Old Cars Weekly
700 East State Street
Iola, WI 54990

Old Cars Price Guide
Same address as Old Cars Weekly (OCW)
A guide, not an official price list to collector/antique cars. Most insurance companies use the guide as a basis for insuring a car.

Cars & Parts
911 Vandemark Road
Sidney, OH 45365

Collectible Automobile
5615 W. Cermak Road
Cicero, IL 60650-2290

Glossary

Bbl: Refers to carburetor's number of barrels (1 bbl/2 bbls).

Bore and Stroke: Diameter of the cylinder and the length of the piston's stroke from top to bottom.

Cid: Cubic inch displacement. Represents the volume size of the engine.

Liter: Metric volume size of engine. One liter is 60.975 cubic inches. One cubic inch equals 16.387 cubic centimenters (cc). 1,000 cc equals one liter.

Coil Springs: Springs coiled in a spiral.

Compression Ratio: The ratio between the volume of the cylinder when the piston is all the way up and when it is all the way down. As combustion space gets smaller the ratios tend to get higher. The higher the compression, the more efficiently the fuel is burned. But this also requires a higher grade of gasoline, which translates into more expensive gasoline. If your car has a ''knock'' in it you need a higher grade of gas or the engine needs retuning.

Coupe: Before the hardtop, this term referred to a sporty two-door.

Dual Exhaust (Twin Exhaust): Two mufflers and two sets of exhaust pipes and resonators. Twice the headaches of a single exhaust (and more money). Very good for exhaust companies!

Dual Quads (Two Fours): Two four-barrel carburetors (2–4 bbls/2–4's).

Fastback: Style of two-door (and some four-door) cars popular in the 1930s and late 1940s. Also known as sedanette. Fastback designs are back in vogue today.

Hardtop: A pillarless car. No posts between front door and rear door and no door frame around the windows on the door. 1949 was the first year of the two-door hardtop (Buick and Cadillac) and 1955 was the year of the first four-door hardtop. The last year for the American hardtop was 1976.

Ind: Independent as in independent suspension.

Cyl: Cylinder as in V-8 cylinder engine.

Hardtop Convertible: Same as the term ''hardtop,'' but somehow has come to be used for two-door hardtop. The only true hardtop convertible was the 1957–1959 Ford Skyliner.

Horsepower: The maximum horsepower an engine will develop under certain laboratory conditions, without such accessories as exhausts, air-conditioning, power equipment (steering, brakes), etc. Optional power equipment can reduce a car's maximum horsepower frrom 25 to 50 percent! All horsepower figures given in this book are brake horsepower (BHP).

Land Yacht: Refers to a big (Buick, Caddy, Lincoln) chrome machine of the 50s.

Leaf Springs: Straight pieces of steel that are given a slight curve and then placed on top of each other. Leaf springs usually give a firmer or stiffer ride than coil springs.

Manual Shift: Transmission with a clutch and stick for changing gears. The stick shift can either be floor-mounted or column-mounted on the steering post. Until the late 1930s all manual shifts were floor-mounted. It was considered a "luxury feature" to have the shift column mounted. Today a floor-mounted shift with a console is a "luxury item." The more things change . . .

Maximum Torque: The amount of turning force exerted at the flywheel by the engine which makes the power wheels turn (rear-wheel or front-wheel drive).

Muscle Car: Relatively lightweight cars with a big engine and heavy-duty suspensions so the cars could handle reasonably well given their power-to-weight ratio.

Pony Car: This is a small sporty car that seats two up front comfortably and two in the rear not so comfortably. The Camaro, Firebird, AMX, Barracuda, Challenger, and Mustang were all pony cars. But we know there is only one real "pony," and that is the Mustang. This is the car that was first and even has a pony right in its grille. The Mustang pony even defies the laws of nature; they breed in captivity. There seem to be more around today than when they were first unveiled to the public in April 1964.

Pop-up Headlights: The 1936 Cord had them. The Cord also had a supercharged V-8 engine and front-wheel drive!

Rear-Axle Ratio: The number of turns of the drive shaft necessary to make both rear wheels (rear-wheel drive) complete one full revolution. The lower the ratio, the fewer the engine rpms and the better the fuel economy (in theory). The larger the ratio, the better the getaway of the car from a stop and the easier the car can go up a steep grade without downshifting.

Shipping Weight: The weight of the car without optional equipment such as air-conditioning, power steering, etc., and without any liquid contents such as gasoline, water, or oil. Curb weight is the car with all optional equipment and all liquids to their proper levels. Unless noted, all cars in the book are in shipping weight.

Supercharged: A mechanical form of Turbo-Charged, using the excess gases and exhaust for more power. The 1929 Duesenberg had a supercharger as well as the 1954 Willys, 1957 Studebaker, and 1957 Thunderbird (known as an F-Bird). A lot of hot air.

Tin or Old Tin: Commonly refers to old cars

Tri-power: Three dual-barrel carburetors. Also known as three deuces, three-two's, and "a six-pack" when on muscle cars (3–2 bbls/3–2's).

Wheelbase: The distance from the center of a front wheel to the center of a rear wheel. Usually the longer the wheelbase, the better or less bouncy the ride.

Yank Tank: What Europeans fondly call American cars from the 50s and 60s. What are known in the United States as "land yachts" or sometimes as cruisers. A cruiser is not necessarily as big as a Buick or Caddy but a cruiser has flash, style, skirts, dice, and should be two-tone. A '55 Ford Crown Victoria or '57 Mercury Turnpike Cruiser are good examples. These are cars that were made for submarine race watching.

General-Interest Car Club Listings

Antique Automobile
  Association of Brooklyn
c/o Michael Graff
824 E. 21st Street
Brooklyn, NY 11210

Antique Automobile Club of
  America
501 W. Governor Rd., PO Box
  417
Hershey, PA 17033

Antique & Classic Car Club of
  Canada
7013 Cadiz Cres.
Mississauga, Ontario
Canada L5N 1Y3

Automobile Collectors Club
  International
Box 4764
New River Stage II
Phoenix, AZ 85027

Canadian Street Rod
  Association
604 River Rd. S.
Peterborough, Ontario
Canada K9J 1E7

Classic Car Club of America
O'Hare Lake Office Plaza
2300 E. Devon Ave., Suite 126
Des Plains, IL 60018

Contemporary Historical
  Vehicle Association
16944 Dearborn St.
Sepulveda, CA 91343

Historical Automobile Society
  of Canada
820 York Road, RR2
Guelph, Ontario
Canada N1H 6H8

Horseless Carriage Club of
  America
7210 Jordan Ave., Box D76
Canoga Park, CA 91303

Milestone Car Society
PO Box 50850
Indianapolis, IN 46250

National Street Rod Association
4030 Park Ave.
Memphis, TN 38111

Society of Automotive
  Historians
Box 514
Mt. Gretna, PA 17064

Veteran Motor Car Club of
  America
18840 Pearl Road
PO Box 36788
Strongsville, OH 44136

About the Author

JAY HIRSCH is a professional photographer and writer, and an automobile consultant and supplier to the movie, TV, and advertising industries. An enthusiastic expert on American automobiles—particularly of the 50s and 60s—he owns nine classic American cars and drives them as often as he can. He lives on the Hudson River in Grand View, New York, where he cruises in his wood-bodied 1959 Owens.